STEAM SUPREME

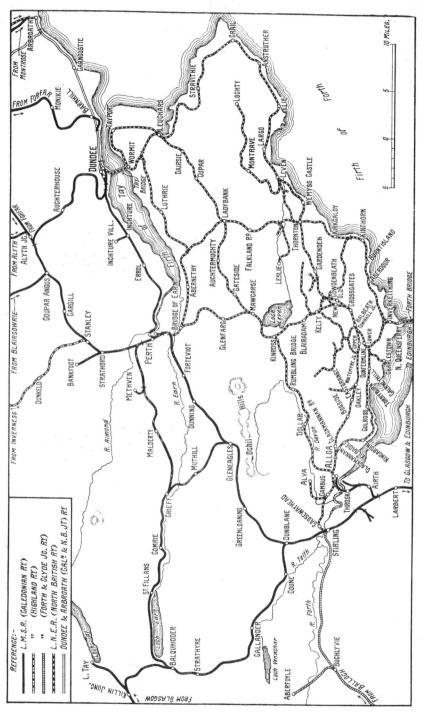

Railways covering the Fife area circa 1928

STEAM SUPREME

recollections of Scottish railways in the 1920s

R. D. STEPHEN

BRADFORD BARTON

ISBN 0 85153 374 4

first published by
D. BRADFORD BARTON LIMITED
TRURO · CORNWALL
© R. D. STEPHEN

printed in Great Britain by
LOVELL BAINES PRINT LTD · NEWBURY · BERKSHIRE

CONTENTS

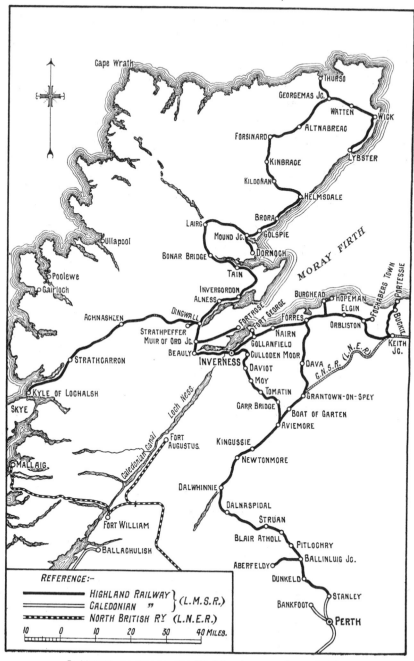

Railways covering the Highland area circa 1928

INTRODUCTION

When I was considering material for this paperback volume about my railway memories of bygone days, there were some initial doubts in my mind as to whether they would be of real interest to the present-day enthusiast, especially in view of the many books published in recent years, which must have left very little untold about railway history during the last half-century. Fortunately, I was greatly encouraged by someone younger, who reminded me that those who had experienced and remembered the railway scene sixty and more years ago were today not very numerous. . . .

Apart from a few references to recent visits to some of my old haunts, the period covered is devoted mostly to the ten years which concluded in 1930, when I left this country for a future life in the Far East. My railway interest remained, but although there were periodical home furloughs continuity was broken, and one often found, for example, after a few years' absence, that old engine friends and even classes had gone forever. Perhaps inevitably, in the circumstances my serious railway photography ceased. Fortunately, not a single copy of the 'Railway Magazine' was lost due to U-boat sinkings on the long voyage round the Cape during the 1939-45 war, when I was working in Aden - and, thanks to this, I was able to keep in touch with railway happenings in the U.K.

My interest in railways was of a general nature, engines for which I had a great affection taking priority, and while their main dimensions were studied, it was largely to enable comparison with their opposite numbers on other railways. Different valve gears and efficient driving techniques meant little to me, possibly influenced by the 'Railway Magazine' monthly articles on 'British Locomotive Practice and Performance', which, fifty years ago, were generally geared chiefly to performance. Footplate passes were not commonplace, and with most train timing being done from the compartment, the layman had little knowledge of any problems in the driver's cab.

I have never attempted to time a train; indeed,

looking back to early Inverkeithing days, I seldom noted
the passing times of those on the Aberdeen and Perth
roads, which always seemed to turn up when they were
expected. The North British was invariably praised for
exemplary timekeeping, and, while the schedules may have
been on the easy side, it was obvious that maximum effort
was required, judging by the energetic way all drivers
tackled the steep gradients, short and otherwise. The
same skill was apparent downhill and on the more level
sections, where numerous curves prevented really fast
running. Nevertheless, the late Cecil J. Allen, renowned
as an expert on locomotives and train working, often
complained about the leisurely progress of N.B. Atlantics
on the suitably straight and level seventeen miles
between Dundee and Arbroath.

The selection of photographs is comprehensive, but
others taken on shed visits and elsewhere, in some cases
referred to in these pages, appear in 'Scottish Steam in
the 1920s' and 'Scottish Steam Miscellany', to which this
book is in the nature of a sequel.

It is hoped that these varied reminiscences will
enable the reader to sense some of the atmosphere of a
most interesting period in British railway history, and
also show how some of us felt about contemporary events
and developments. For the writer, it is difficult to
credit that it all happened such a long time ago.

Ranald D. Stephen

Bolton-le-Sands, Carnforth

I
EARLY DAYS

My first childhood interest in railways was inevitable, with the North British Railway main line from
Edinburgh to Aberdeen passing so close to my birthplace
- The Manse at Inverkeithing. This was situated on the
hillside overlooking Inverkeithing Bay, and had a perfect
grandstand view of the railway's steep climb to Ferryhills and the Forth Bridge. The Reid Atlantics were
noted for their loud voices, and to see and hear them
tackling the 1 in 70 gradient must have been very
thrilling to a small boy - as it was to his seniors. It
was regarded as a great treat to be taken to the garden
wall to see what became known in the family as 'Big
Aberdeen Puffies'. As time passed, the N.B. Atlantics
became universally famous, and they remained firm favourites of mine until they passed on in the 1930s. Sad it
was that No.875 'Midlothian', restored from partial
scrapping for preservation, became a victim in the search
for scrap metal soon after the outbreak of the war in
September 1939.
My earliest experiences of train travel are associated
with 1915, the second year of the first world war, when
schooldays commenced at the Edinburgh Academy Prep',
entailing a daily return journey to Edinburgh of 26
miles. This, for me, was to continue for another fifteen
years. Consequently, the liking for trains developed,
and I have some clear memories of those days, not least
of the train which took us to and from school.
Starting its inward journey at Ladybank, it picked us
up at Inverkeithing at 7.55 a.m., arriving at Waverley
at 8.31 a.m., having called at North Queensferry,
Dalmeny, Turnhouse and Saughton, and, of course,
Haymarket. Saughton and Turnhouse stations were closed
many years ago.
Homeward bound, we left Waverley at 3.50 p.m. with
the same rolling stock, engine and crew, the latter
booking off during the daytime, their engine being
usefully employed working empty coaching stock around
Edinburgh. Inevitably, the 'school train' became a real
family affair, and its regular driver, Tommy Thompson
from Ladybank shed, was a great favourite, who made

certain that no boy missed an invitation to the footplate
of his Holmes 4-4-0 (No.636) while the train was awaiting
departure from platform Number Ten.

The coaches, a mixture of four- and six-wheeled stock
built in the 1880s, were very primitive indeed, particularly as regards their heating and lighting. The former
was provided by 'footwarmers', large galvanised pans
containing a heat-retaining chemical, which after
thorough heating in vast steaming cauldrons situated
under the inclined carriage entrance to the Waverley were
very deftly slid into each compartment by two porters
using hooks. If the seats were already occupied, passengers had to raise their feet while this was being done.
One recalls the unpleasant steam, if the floor was wet -
invariably the case in winter; and also how quickly the
heating system cooled down.

Lighting was by gas jet burners or oil lamps. In the
former case, the supply having been turned on at the end
of the coach, each compartment was lit individually by a
porter with a large flaming torch, the whole operation
attended by a strong smell of escaped gas, until the
lamps were lit. The oil lamps, already lit, were
trundled along the platform nesting in specially
constructed barrows heaved up by a porter on the coach
roof, who inserted them in the openings of each compartment, replacing each lamp top with a loud bang. In mid-
winter we could be sitting in semi-darkness, relieved
only by the station arc lamps, waiting for light and
heat - all very incongruous in a station whose extensive
modernisation had been completed barely twelve years
earlier. A year or two after I started travelling, oil
lamps and jet burners gave place to incandescent gas
lighting as well as steam heating, although many years
were to pass before the 'school train' was promoted to
bogie stock.

The 3.50 was a merry train, little patronised by
adults, and 'empty' compartments were plentiful. A
favourite game was to stand astride the seats as the
train almost bounced over the trailing crossover at
Turnhouse station - which was adjacent to an air force
aerodrome (now Edinburgh Airport), the aim being to
maintain one's balance without clutching the luggage
racks. This was not at all easy for the short-legged;
while another vivid memory is of small boys who had
displeased their seniors being banished to the luggage

racks for their entire journey.

Haymarket shed was a major attraction, and in the
final years of the war there was an armoured train lying
in a siding at Saughton, a four-platformed station
serving both Fife and Glasgow lines. One of two armoured
trains commissioned by the War Office at the outbreak of
the war for coastal defence in Berwickshire and Kincar-
dineshire, it was made up of an engine and tender,
marshalled between four bogie vans. Those at the ends
had open gun platforms mounted with what were probably
eighteen-pounder guns in naval-type shields, the entire
train being heavily steel-plated. The engine, barely
recognisable, was one of Ivatt's Great Northern N.1
0-6-2Ts, with a tender augmenting the water supply.
Coaling and servicing was attended to at Haymarket shed,
the engine leaving its train in the siding for this
purpose.

Another special treat was seeing the Royal Train in
its L.N.W.R. umber and white livery standing in a siding
            ny, indicating that King George V and Queen Mary
were paying a visit to the Grand Fleet at Rosyth.

A final memory of over sixty years ago was being taken
to the scene of the Burntisland Railway disaster on
14 April 1914, involving the night Kings Cross - Aberdeen
express, which left Waverley in the early morning hours.
Atlantic No.872 'Auld Reekie' overran a home signal and
struck a goods engine which had nearly completed backing
its train over a trailing crossover from the up to the
down line. The glancing blow overturned the Atlantic
onto its side in the sand of the golf links, with the
tender jackknifing the cab, killing both driver and
fireman. High speed was not a factor, in view of the
speed restrictions over the sharp reverse curves for
which Burntisland is noted; nevertheless, there was
telescoping, and considerable damage to the leading
coaches, but no further fatal casualties. Views of the
accident, which received great press publicity, were
recorded by a local professional photographer, and one of
these, reproduced here, shows how deeply the Atlantic
buried herself in the sand, and the terrible consequences
of the jackknifing of tender and engine. In the background is the old roundhouse shed of the Edinburgh, Perth
& Dundee Railway, which was formed in 1849.

Prior to the completion of the Forth Bridge in 1890,
Burntisland was an important link in the East Coast Route

from the south to Aberdeen, being the northern railhead
of the Firth of Forth ferry service from Granton. The
ferry service, which commenced in 1844, was absorbed by
the North British Railway in 1862, and finally by the
L.N.E.R. in 1923. Particularly famous on the run was the
paddle steamer, 'William Muir', built at Kinghorn in
1879, which apart from acting as a mine-sweeper from 1917
to 1919 - the ferry service being suspended during the
war period - was continually on the Granton - Burntisland
run until withdrawn in 1937. Replacing it was the
'Snowdrop', an ex-Mersey ferry, which was renamed 'Thane
of Fife' and ran until March 1940, when the service was
suspended. It is interesting to see from a contemporary
report that passengers travelling from the Dundee direction were once again transferred to the ferry on its very
last day, due to both lines between Inverkeithing and
North Queensferry being blocked by the derailment of two
goods trains. In my early schooldays I frequently
travelled home on the 'Willie Muir', as it was affect-
ionately called, as fortunately when the Forth Bridge
route was opened, it was stipulated that the fare from
Edinburgh to Burntisland via the shorter sea route was
not to be proportionately increased for the considerably
longer mileage - albeit quicker transport - via Dalmeny
and the new bridge. Consequently, the same fare from
Waverley applied to all stations north of the bridge as
far as Burntisland, and it was customary to buy a season
for maximum distance. This was an interesting example of
the intracacies of fare structures.

When war censorship ended in 1919, my father decided
to buy a camera, with the intention of taking photographs
of the naval ships lying in the Forth, which had interested us so much for four long years. In the event, it
was quite unsuitable, for the intended subjects were
lying much too far offshore, but it was this camera that
started my collection of railway photographs. It was a
very simple folding pocket camera with three shutter
speeds and 'Time', described as a 1A Junior Kodak, with a
very suitable picture size of 2½" x 4¼". Anastigmatic
lens were somewhat uncommon and certainly expensive in
those days, but fortunately the camera chosen had the
next best lens available, a pre-war Kodak Doublet. As
the name signifies, this was a double lens, one combination in front and one behind the diaphragm. Known also
as the Rapid Rectilinear (R.R.), the stops were marked in

the 'Uniform System' (U.S.), in which the numbers were
proportional to the exposure required. The largest stop
was U.S. 4, being equivalent to f8, at which with 1/25th
second many of my photographs were taken - except in the
most ideal conditions, when U.S. 8, f11, could be used.
Apart from slight lack of sharpness at the edges,
definition was excellent - in fact, the R.R. lens gave
far better results than a Kodak Anastigmatic, for which
it was exchanged in 1924.

Kodak film was described as 'non-curling', apparently
of some market value, as the letters 'N' and 'C' were
prominently featured on the familiar yellow carton.
Speed was slow, and its general quality was very aptly
described in a Kodak manual of later years as 'trans-
parent', compared with 'translucent', in the case of the
new Verichrome film. Amateur photography, especially
with film, was of course very much in its infancy at this
date, whilst commercial developing and printing left a
lot to be desired. However, with modern enlarging
techniques, prints from these old negatives are very
satisfactory, and remarkably free of grain. As a matter
of interest, the cost of one print inclusive of film and
processing was sevenpence (3p) - quite expensive over
fifty years ago.

Another event in 1919 which changed my interest in
railway from mere watching the trains go by to something
more positive was that, after war service, my brother,
W.D.M. Stephen, joined the N.B.R. headquarters staff at
Waterloo Place, Edinburgh, under W.A. Fraser, the
engineer-in-chief. Here he had access to the official
engine diagrams, and as soon as he became proficient with
a draughtsman's pen, he commenced taking tracings of the
outline drawings of all the N.B. locomotive classes.
These, at a scale of one-quarter inch to one foot,
included basic dimensions and numbers in each class. It
is interesting that the last tracing is from the diagram
of a Gresley Pacific, sent by H.N. Gresley from Doncaster
early in 1923, when permission was being sought for
No.1481N, suitably adapted for the restricted Scottish
loading gauge, to run trials between Newcastle and
Edinburgh. For the first time, we had an up-to-date and
accurate detailed history of the North British locomotive
stock.

This was invaluable at a time when the railway
companies - particularly in some cases - were reluctant

to release details of their building programmes, or
advance lists of numbers (and names, when they applied),
although the stringencies of the war were in some degree
responsible for this. On the other hand, there was
always the element of the unexpected at shed visits and
observations along the line. Two stand out, the first
seeing, quite unexpectedly, a Great Western 2-8-0,
No.2804, passing north through Inverkeithing about 1921.
I learned some time afterwards that it had been engaged
in comparative trials with a North British Class S 0-6-0
on the Glenfarg bank, a few miles south of Perth. The
other was seeing for the first time the quite incredible
name 'Wandering Willie' on North British superheated
'Scott' No.499.

One main source of railway information was of course
the 'Railway Magazine', first published in July 1897 and
monthly thereafter. There was also the 'Locomotive
Magazine', published by the Locomotive Publishing Co.,
whose home at 3 Amen Corner, E.C.2, disappeared in the
Blitz of the Second World War. Costing two pennies -
almost invisible in decimal currency - a typical copy,
dated 15 October 1915, provided 22 well-informed pages,
with fourteen engine photographs, eight engine line
drawings, in addition to a number of diagrams of sundry
components. Inflation must have been dormant in those
days, as the price had remained unaltered since 1897.
In this particular issue, there is a full page advertisement by the Superheater Corporation Ltd., enticing
locomotive superintendents to save 25 per cent of their
fuel bills by installing a Robinson superheater.
Accompanying sundry details is the assurance that 'the
Robinson superheater never leaks' (and the 'never' was
even in italics). This of course was the period in
locomotive history when the superheater was coming into
its own, and any engine so equipped was regarded by a
young enthusiast with great respect, almost awe,
although generally the only outward sign was a slightly
longer smokebox of exactly the same shape as before
and, not invariably, a mechanical lubricator. Non-
superheated engines were small fry by comparison. The
drive from the piston crosshead to the mechanical
lubricator of the North British Atlantic - very evident
in my photograph of 'Thane of Fife' on page 14 of
'Scottish Steam Miscellany' - did help to offset the
Walschaerts valve gear on the Caledonian 'River' and

Pickersgill three-cylinder 4-6-0s, of which we were
extremely jealous. In retrospect, all rather childish -
but that is how we felt.

Another monthly the more elderly will remember was the
'Railway & Travel Monthly'. Launched by G.A. Sekon, who
had just relinquished the editorship of the 'Railway
Magazine', this also cost sixpence, but as the title
indicated, it also covered shipping, aviation and motor
transport. Its railway coverage was excellent for a
time, not least of which were some beautiful colour
plates, but this coverage declined in 1920 when, to
broaden its scope, the title was changed to 'Transport &
Travel Monthly', eventually merging with the 'Railway'
Magazine' in 1923.

There was also a little fortnightly called the
'Locomotive News', the first issue appearing on 10 March
1919. This paper welcomed any information about engine
numbers, locations, particularly of newly-built types.
Although not always entirely accurate - due possibly to
printer's errors - it was pleasant to read nonetheless,
and considerably more informal than the somewhat conservative 'Railway Magazine'. Another of its policies was
to publish photographs taken by lesser mortals than the
well-known F.E. Mackay, H.Gordon Todey, Rixon Bucknall,
etc., and it was in the 'Locomotive News' that the work
of many of the well-known railway photographers of later
years first appeared. Benefitting from its fortnightly
publication, it was first on the scene with an illustra-
tion of the new Gresley Pacific No.1470 'Great Northern'.

Also available to the enthusiast were the splendid
postcard series and beautiful oil paintings bearing the
name F. Moore, published by the Locomotive Publishing
Co. As regards Scotland, the Highland and North British
Railways were very well represented, largely due to the
efforts of a Major Munro at Perth. This series, however,
had ceased in 1914, and while the various publications
did their best to illustrate new war-built engines or
interesting rebuilds, frequently they had to be content
with official works photographs of grey-painted engines
with black-and-white lining. The fact is that there
were few railway photographers at the time, although the
rapid post-war development of the cheaper film camera
soon had its effect. Indeed, I had no serious competi-
tors in this respect for several years. One had to reach
a high standard to get into the pages of the 'Railway

Magazine', due to some extent to the poor style of paper
then used; in fact, it was not until the mid-1930s that
this periodical commenced using art paper for its
illustrations.

Inverkeithing, thirteen miles north of Edinburgh on
the main line and the junction for the Aberdeen and Perth
lines, was an ideal place to start with a camera. There
was plenty of still life available, moving subjects -
except at the slowest speeds - being then beyond the
scope of the camera shutter. The layout was spacious
and, oriented north and south, provided suitable sunlit
subjects in the earlier part of the day and all afternoon. A brief summary will give some idea of the train
service in the N.B.'s final days.

First in importance was the Aberdeen line.
Northbound, the first train was one we never saw, this
being the night sleeper from Kings Cross with a through
carriage from Penzance attached, which went through about
three in the morning. Next was the 7.35 a.m. from
Waverley with through coaches from Kings Cross, including
two sleeping cars, also five M. & N.B. corridors from
St. Pancras via the Waverley Route. These were normal
Midland clerestory style lettered M. & N.B. With one of
the heavy steel dining cars, plus N.B. portion from
Waverley, this was a heavy train, and its Atlantic was
always assisted by a Holmes 4-4-0. On Sundays there was
also the Penzance coach, there being no all-night
sleeping car train from Kings Cross at the weekend. A
'Scott' was then rostered as pilot.

The four other trains for Aberdeen from Waverley were
the 10.15 a.m. with a through carriage for Elgin on the
Great North, one of their lake-and-white coaches working
on alternate days with a N.B. composite. Followed the
2.15 p.m. and then the 4.25 p.m., a semi-fast which
stopped at Inverkeithing largely because of its proximity
to Rosyth Dockyard. It might be added here that the
station name boards read 'Inverkeithing for Rosyth Dockyard': Rosyth Halt on the Perth line catered more for
the residential area nearby, then known as Rosyth Garden
City. Finally, there was the 6.35 p.m. with through
coaches, ex the 10 a.m. from Kings Cross - it is
difficult to avoid using the title 'Flying Scotsman', but
this train had not received official recognition at that
time.

Southbound from Aberdeen a train left around 6 a.m.,

taking the through Kings Cross coaches to join the
10 a.m. ex-Waverley. Remaining departures were the
9.45 a.m. with the Penzance coach, the 12.50 a.m. with
the coach from Elgin, and the 3.40 p.m., which was the
return working of the 10.15 from Waverley. The last two
trains were the 5.45 p.m. with the St. Pancras portion,
the day ending with the 7.15 p.m. night sleeper to Kings
Cross. In high summer there was sufficient daylight to
see this on its stiff climb up to Ferryhills, making a
delightful end to an evening at one of our favourite
haunts. All these trains were of course Atlantic-hauled,
with a pilot as necessary. The appropriate maximum loads
for an Atlantic were as follows:

Edinburgh-Aberdeen   475 tons
    (through loads, assisted throughout)
Edinburgh-Aberdeen   370 tons
    (through loads, unassisted)
Aberdeen-Edinburgh   475 tons
    (through loads, assisted throughout)
Aberdeen-Dundee   340 tons
    (through loads, unassisted. The lesser load,
    unassisted, was probably due to the start on
    the steep bank from Stonehaven)
Dundee-Edinburgh   370 tons
    (through loads, unassisted. With the proviso
    that assistance had to be taken to the Forth
    Bridge, if stopped at Inverkeithing)

Understandably, the service to and from Perth corres-
ponded generally to those on the Aberdeen route, most
providing similar connections with the south. These were
in charge of superheated 'Scotts', with the exception of
a double trip each day by a St. Margaret's Atlantic.
Other main line passenger trains to be seen were semi-
fast and stopping trains to or from Dundee and Stirling,
as well as between Glasgow (Queen Street) and Dundee.
In spite of such a busy timetable, only four north
stopping trains were suitable for the camera, southbound
being a little better with six. Unfortunately - and to
my subsequent regret - I avoided taking photographs with
the platform as a foreground; J.P. Gairns, editor of the
'Railway Magazine' for many years, made it very clear
that he did not generally favour these, unless there was
something of exceptional interest in addition to the train

itself, or to illustrate his series of articles entitled
'Notable Railway Stations and their Traffic'.

On the credit side, there were numerous locals from
Thornton and Dunfermline suitably connecting with trains
on the coast and Perth lines; their engines could always
be photographed when they were taking water and cleaning
fires. Further material was provided by the goods loops,
which were invariably occupied whilst there was always
the little colony of banking engines on constant duty on
the three gradients - Forth Bridge to the south, Dalgety
on the Aberdeen line, and Townhill Junction on the Perth.
These were mainly Wheatley 0-6-0s, built over a period
from 1867, and rebuilt successively by Holmes and Reid.
For a long time, these included No.1162, No.1222, No.1223
and No.1166. Assisting them at times were Holmes West
Highland 4-4-0s, which were nearing the end of their
days, plus No.1249, a little 2-4-0 by Wheatley, also with
two rebuildings to its credit.

Nevertheless, with the vagaries of the sun, steam and
smoke which blew in the wrong direction, and the
perpetual problem of slow films, it took a long time to
build up a collection, even with the aid of long school
holidays. The N.B. did not move their engines about much
as regards shed allocations, and the same ones could be
seen on the same train for many months, sometimes years.

Edinburgh Waverley, or the 'Waverley' as it was known
locally, was second only to Waterloo as the largest
station in Great Britain. Its complete modernisation,
together with the building of the North British Station
Hotel, which dominates Princes Street, was completed in
1902. It was a perfect example of a railway terminus
when I first became familiar with it, and one of which
we were justly proud. Unfortunately, owing to the very
ample platform umbrella roofing, it was no place for
photography of stationary subjects, but nevertheless it
was always an exciting place to visit during busy times.

A regular Saturday morning expedition during school
term was into Edinburgh with the 8.05 a.m. from Inverkeithing, the connection from Perth connecting with the
night service from Inverness to Glasgow. Stopping at
every station, it was invariably hauled by superheated
'Scott' No.418 'Dumbiedykes', which together with No.270
'Glen Garry' was a Perth engine. Having reached
Waverley, the first evidence of the morning departures
for London was the sight of three North Eastern engines

passing through to the east end from Haymarket shed: two
Raven Z Atlantics for the London trains, the 10 a.m.
(once again, not then called the 'Flying Scotsman'), and
the 10.15 a.m., plus a Worsdell Class R 4-4-0, rostered
for the 10.25 a.m. semi-fast to York, made up of non-
vestibuled North Eastern corridor stock, a mixture of
clerestory and elliptical-roofed. We were always a
little jealous of the bright green livery of the North
Eastern, having to admit very discreetly that the N.B.
livery was a shade dingy by comparison. On the other
hand, we were somewhat contemptuous about the Raven
Atlantics, which sounded a little stuffy with their soft
three-cylinder exhaust, so different from our Reid
Atlantics, which made no bones about it, and really
cleared their throats.

Connecting with the southbound trains were expresses
from Aberdeen, Glasgow and Perth, all of which brought
through carriages for the 10 a.m. I have a note that
one particular day the Aberdeen train came in with
Atlantic No.874 'Dunedin' from Glasgow, Eastfield superheated 'Scott' No.413 'Laird o' Monkbarns', and the last
to arrive, No.270 'Glen Garry' from Perth, all providing
nice examples of the splendid variety of engine names on
the N.B.

Frequently, during the high season, the 10 a.m. had
one of the Class R 4-4-0s as pilot, but this was all to
change a few years later with the advent of the Gresley
Pacifics. The train of course was primarily of Great
Northern design, Gresley being the author - all very
smart in varnished teak, lined in red and yellow, and
lettered E.C.J.S., indicating that it was the joint stock
of the three partners: G.N., N.E. and N.B. An interesting feature was the all-steel kitchen car, two of
which were built in 1914, which must have been the first
passenger stock to be painted in simulated teak,
anticipating what became universal after the Grouping.

The next departure for the south was the 10.05 a.m.
for St. Pancras, consisting of Midland-built clerestory
carriages jointly owned by the two companies, and
lettered M. & N.B. This was in charge of a Carlisle
Atlantic, which had arrived at Waverley in the early
hours, with the sleeping car train from St. Pancras.
Frequently the engine concerned was No.906 'Teribus'.

The 10.15 a.m. southbound was probably the most
interesting, and certainly the most diverse, of the day.

During the summer months it ran through to Kings Cross as
a relief to the 10 a.m., but throughout the year it
conveyed as far as York a through service from Glasgow
(Queen Street) to Southampton and Harwich. The former
portion consisted of two coaches, Great Central and Great
Western, on alternate days, while a Great Eastern
composite sufficed for Harwich. Their distinctive
liveries were a striking addition to the remainder of the
varnished teak formation. In winter, with the addition
of a few coaches and a diner at Edinburgh, the train
terminated at York.

Returning to the west end, there was the 10 a.m. to
Queen Street with a superheated 'Scott', frequently
No.409 'The Pirate', followed by the 10.05 a.m. to Perth
with 'Dumbiedykes', which had brought me in from Inverkeithing a short time earlier. Finally, there was the
10.15 a.m. to Aberdeen,with its through coach for Elgin.
This little expedition, providing so much variety,
concluded with a run home on the 10.25 a.m. slow for
Dundee behind saturated 'Scott' No.361 'Vich Ian Vhor'.

I had a great affection for the Waverley. As the
years passed, it became very grimy, and it is pleasant
to see it again now thoroughly modernised, with a
completely new and up-to-date layout. It may be no
Euston or New Street, but it has a character, and
remains a worthy tribute to its first owners. A major
change is that only two dock platforms remain at the
east end, the area having been adapted for the handling
of parcels and mails. One reflects nostalgically on the
trains that ran to Musselburgh and such places as
Lasswade, Polton and Penicuik.

With no season ticket available during the school
holidays, Edinburgh, however, was practically a closed
book. Cycling there was more or less out of the
question, as the privately-owned and somewhat ancient
paddler named 'Woolwich', on the Forth ferry service,
was very slow and tedious to use. Thus, most of the
long summer holidays were spent at Inverkeithing, with
occasional cycle trips to Stirling and Perth.

An interesting little bywater near at hand was the
Kirkcaldy Harbour branch. With a ruling gradient of
1 in 20, it was worked by Reid's little 0-6-0Ts, with
outside cylinders and dumb buffers, known in later
years as Class J.88. The directions in the official
manual of maximum loads on the branch are most

interesting:

> The Maximum load will be as follows:-
>   8 loaded mineral wagons and incline brake or
>   10 loaded goods wagons and incline brake or
>   6 loaded bulk grain vans and incline brake.
> In cases of unfavourable circumstances, to ensure
> safety, the above loads may be reduced to an
> extent governed by the judgment and discretion of
> the Enginemen and Guard in charge of the train.
> In the event of a difference of opinion, the
> smaller number of wagons contended for by either
> of these men to constitute the train load.
>   The engine must always be at the lower end of
> the wagons and the speed must not exceed 4 miles
> per hour.

Many years later, in November 1954, J.88 No.68341 ran out
of control down the gradient with nineteen loaded wagons,
an excess of seven over the then permitted load,
resulting in the J.88 and some of its train disappearing
below the water. It was fished up and withdrawn from
service, the first of the class to be withdrawn.

Another line often visited and of great historical
interest was the Fordell Railway, a six-mile colliery
line connecting pits in the neighbourhood of Crossgates
(on the N.B. main line to Perth) with the small port of
St. Davids, a few miles east of Inverkeithing. Dating
back to a wooden wagonway built about 1770, it developed
into line with malleable iron rails worked by horses, and
finally became steam-worked in 1867. The unusual gauge
of 4' 4" dated back to its earliest period, and necessitated some rather complicated point work where it
connected with the standard gauge at the pits. The two
engines I remember were 'Alice', built by Grant Ritchie
& Co. of Kilmarnock in 1880, and 'Lord Hobart', built by
Barclays in 1912. Both were 0-4-0 saddle tanks. The
wagons were of the cauldron type, devoid of any springs,
and with an empty weight of 30cwts and a coal-carrying
capacity of 48cwts. The last load to be delivered to a
steam 'puffer' at St. Davids was on 10 August 1946.
Unfortunately, I took no photographs of this unique line,
traces of which may be seen alongside the road from
St. Davids to the A92. Near to the road junction is the
bridge which carried the Fordell Railway under the main
line to Aberdeen.

Cowlairs was very conservative in their locomotive designs, both passenger and goods classes being developed from Dugald Drummond's engines of the last century. They culminated in Reid's very capable superheated 'Scotts' and 'Glens', as well as his most successful heavy 0-6-0 - more simply identified for the present-day reader as Class J.37. Exceptional of course were the Atlantics, originating in 1906, finally totalling 22 in number. Various writers have tried to convey their appeal and majestic appearance, but to me they were simply the premier engines of my favourite railway. Moreover, they were good to look at; the 5' 6" diameter boiler, with a centre line 8' 11" above rail level, and an even larger diameter smokebox, combined with the restricted loading gauge, necessitated what must have been the lowest boiler mounting then in existence. These, especially the low and shapely funnel, were the features which first caught the eye. Their names were:

No.868 'Aberdonian'	No.879 'Abbotsford'
No.869 'Bonnie Dundee'	No.880 'Tweeddale'
(formerly 'Dundonian')	No.881 'Borderer'
No.870 'Bon-Accord'	No.901 'St.Johnstoun'
No.871 'Thane of Fife'	No.902 'Highland Chief'
No.872 'Auld Reekie'	No.903 'Cock o' the North'
No.873 'Saint Mungo'	No.904 'Holyrood'
No.874 'Dunedin'	No.905 'Buccleuch'
No.875 'Midlothian'	No.906 'Teribus'
No.876 'Waverley'	No.509 'Duke of Rothesay'
No.877 'Liddesdale'	No.510 'The Lord Provost'
No.878 'Hazeldean'	

Most names represented the territory in which they ran, and are easily identifiable; others call for some explanation. 'Bon Accord' is the motto of Aberdeen - the origin supposedly being that it was a cry used by the citizens in 1803 when expelling the English garrison, while 'Saint Mungo' and 'St.Johnstoun' are the patron saints of Glasgow and Perth respectively. In addition to 'Dunedin', Edinburgh's old name, the Scottish capital was also represented by 'Auld Reekie' - a reference to the many smoking chimneys seen from the top of Arthur's Seat in the old days. 'Duke of Rothesay' is the Scottish title of the heir to the throne. Probably the most puzzling to many is 'Teribus', the first word in the motto of Hawick, 'Teribus, ye Teri Odin', the origin of

which is obscure. According to one guide book, the local
people are called Terries, and 'Teribus' is used as a cry
during the Common Ridings.

Several of the Atlantic names were perpetuated on
various L.N.E.R.-designed Pacifics, whilst 'Borderer',
'Thane of Fife' and 'Cock o' the North' may now be seen
on British Rail Class 87 electrics, running on the West
Coast main line - rather oddly described as 'Royal Scot'
Class. Deciphering their names today as they pass my
present home at Bolton-le-Sands, with speeds well into
the nineties, is not as simple a matter as it was with
the Scottish originals so many years ago.

The Reid Atlantic looked splendid freshly turned out
in N.B. passenger colour, but it was a livery that soon
toned down to a somewhat indeterminate shade of drab
green, which tended to dwarf the subject. The visual
impact of seeing an N.E. Raven Atlantic alongside an
N.B. Atlantic, both in L.N.E.R. green, proved this
admirably, the latter definitely appearing the larger and
certainly more impressive of the two. The N.B. livery
was finally described as bronze green, but it did vary in
hue, sometimes with a brownish tendency whilst at others
green predominated. My first view of No.256 'Glen
Douglas' in the Glasgow Transport Museum was quite
breathtaking, for it completely recaptured the North
British engine as I knew it.

Quite a few artists have been successful in portraying
this very perplexing colour, and model makers should be
wary about the extraordinary variation in shades produced
by colour photography. Cowlairs was sparing with the
paint but their engines were kept spotlessly clean, and
a classic example was No.415 'Claverhouse', which had its
name on one side completely rubbed away.

The Railway Year Book gives the N.B.R. locomotive
stock at the end of 1921 as:

Tender:	22	4-4-2	Tank:	51	4-4-2
	192	4-4-0		33	4-4-0
	6	2-4-0		112	0-6-0
	549	0-6-0		75	0-6-2
	1	0-4-0		30	0-4-4
				36	0-4-0

Their total of 1,107 engines exceeded the rival Caledonian by forty at this same period.

Coming to passenger rolling stock, a vestibuled

corridor design 58' 4" long by 8' 6" wide, with high
elliptical roof, was built in 1906 to partner the Reid
Atlantic and provided the standard pattern right through
to the Grouping. They were built to compete on the
Aberdeen services with the Caledonian Grampian Corridor
Express twelve-wheelers, and were luxuriously fitted.
Initially, they came out in blocks of seven, four from
Waverley and three from Glasgow (Queen Street). Connections were made at Dundee on the northward run and at
Dalmeny on the return. In later years the through
coaches from Queen Street to Aberdeen continued even into
Grouping days, the Glasgow train running ahead as a semi-
fast to Dundee. Southwards the Glasgow train was again
in the lead from Dundee to Dalmeny. Running into a loop
at Dalmeny, it then backed on to the coaches from
Aberdeen which had been dropped during a brief stop by
the train for Edinburgh. This provided one of the few
places to photograph a stationary Atlantic in perfect
conditions.

Although additions had been made to the corridor stock
since those built in 1906, the originals were showing
signs of age - evident from the obvious sag in their
frames. This was taken in hand by the L.N.E.R., new
frames being provided and the internal furnishings of the
compartments completely renovated. They ran thereafter
for a long time, and I remember finding one at Kings
Cross on a midday relief to Edinburgh in 1950, link-
coupled between a Gresley Pacific tender and a train of
buckeye standard stock. I was the only passenger in the
coach and it was a pretty rough passage, which I thoroughly enjoyed. A large can of water at each end
provided an important feature of the plumbing - that
coach was getting on in years. Chalmers was responsible
for additions to the carriage fleet, but the internal
compartment panelling with mirrors and pictures was
replaced with ordinary tongue-and-groove partitions,
which rather surprisingly also applied to the prestige
through - first/third van composites built for the
Aberdeen - Penzance service. The carriage headboard of
this through service, the longest in Great Britain and
involving the North British, North Eastern, Great Central
and Great Western Railways, read: 'Aberdeen and Penzance
via Edinburgh York Sheffield Leicester Swindon and
Plymouth'.

We once joined one of these coaches at Nottingham

(Victoria) after two busy days of shed visits and found, in addition to the spartan decor, that the only way of dimming the lights was a felt cover which hinged over the electric bulbs, grouped in a glass globe of the style usually associated with incandescent gas lighting. It was not a restful journey, as the shade kept slipping out of place; moreover, we were late at York and missed the night sleeper from Kings Cross to Aberdeen. Notwith-standing, we were worked forward to Edinburgh as a special in company with six horseboxes, arriving at the Waverley at 5 a.m. Home to Inverkeithing with the 5.50 a.m., and then back to the office in the normal way. One had to work for one's photographs in those days!

The former North British invalid saloon, now owned by the Scottish Railway Preservation Society, is representa-tive of the shape of the final N.B. main line coach. In its days as an invalid saloon, it was always kept under cover in the dock platform at Haymarket station. Apart from being splendidly appointed, with a large bedroom and full-sized bed, there was a compartment for attendants and other necessary facilities. By no means common on Britain's railways, we could never understand why the N.B. thought it necessary to have one.

Pre-1906 stock by Holmes had a flat roof with sharply arced corners, and were simply developments of the earlier six- and four-wheelers. They were somewhat similar to those to be found on the L.S.W.R. - once again the Dugald Drummond influence.

Restaurant cars, always termed dining carriages, first appeared in 1907 from Cowlairs to partner the new sets of corridors of the previous year. Two 66-foot vehicles with six-wheel bogies were built. They were ordinary first and third compartment coaches with two compartments in the centre adapted into a small kitchen, meals being served in the compartments on portable tables. I recall last seeing them in use as diners when the 'Lothian Coast Express', the through business train between Glasgow and the Forth Sea resorts of Dunbar, North Berwick and Gullane, made its first appearance after the war. This train commenced running in 1912 and was composed of three sections. The first departure was about 8 a.m. from Dunbar, with a stop at Drem to pick up the North Berwick portion, which included a dining carriage. Finally, a stop at Longniddry Junction completed the train with two coaches from Gullane, which after a brief stop at

Waverley reached Queen Street at 9.49 a.m. In the afternoon the 'Lothian Coast Express' left Queen Street at
3.50 p.m., just ahead of the 4 p.m. Glasgow - Leeds
express (later to be named the 'North Briton'), its
arrivals being 5.34 p.m. at Gullane, 5.40 p.m. at North
Berwick, and 5.45 p.m. at Dunbar. It was suspended
during the war and reappeared again in 1921. After a
year or two, the kitchens in these two original dining
carriages were converted into small first class coupes
and as such ran for many more years - the only six-
wheeled bogie coaches on the N.B., apart from restaurant
cars.

There were only eleven restaurant cars on the North
British, but they were an interesting and varied
collection. The earliest were two twelve-wheelers,
ex-East Coast stock, with clerestory roofs, purchased
in 1905, which were joined in 1922 by a more modern
one which was finished in varnished teak, retaining the
buckeye coupling and vestibule evidently in anticipation of the imminent Grouping. Hired from the North
Eastern Railway but bearing the lettering of their
present operators were two eight-wheeled cars - short,
with pronounced bulging sides and clerestory roofs.
In 1922 they found their way to the Great North of
Scotland, the first restaurant cars to run on that
railway. Many will remember seeing them in service
between Aberdeen and Inverness, then of course in teak
finish.

Finally came the all-steel diners by Cravens in 1919.
Six in number, there were three different patterns,
68' 11$\frac{5}{8}$" in length and ranging in weight from 45tons
18cwts to 48tons 10cwts, and so the heaviest passenger
vehicles in the country. They were massive-looking
also, with bulging sides, their maximum width being
9', necessitating recessed doors. Rivet heads were
plentiful, and a nice feature was mounting the attractive N.B. crest on wooden plaques, two on each side of
the cars. Internally, like the rest of the post-war
stock, they were austere, with rattan seats in the third
class which always felt very slippery.

Three of the cars were first and third kitchen for
the Aberdeen trains, while for the Glasgow service two
had very ample third class seating with a large kitchen
at one end. Attached to one of them was the sixth, a
first class open saloon with four ordinary first class

compartments at one end. The other third on the Glasgow
run was accompanied by an elderly flat-roofed saloon of
East Coast origin. The steel diners caused a mild
sensation, and I well remember my first trip on one of
them on the 7.35 a.m. from Edinburgh to Aberdeen. One
had to join this at Kirkcaldy, and as there was no
connecting local along the coast at this particular time
we had to take a Dunfermline local as far as Rosyth Halt,
changing to a train from Dunfermline to Thornton which
bypassed Inverkeithing via the North to East Junction
loop. It was thrilling to pass into the diner for breakfast and to feel the wheel taps of a six-wheeled bogie,
so rare in our part of the country. An interesting point
in one of the L.N.E.R. official lists of passenger stock
is that the first class steel with neither kitchen nor
pantry is tabled as a dining carriage, all other catering
vehicles bearing the title restaurant car in accordance
with the practice of the new company.

By 1922, its final year, the N.B. presented quite a
smart appearance. Most of the arrears of maintenance due
to the war had been made up, including repainting of
stations in the standard shades of brown and cream, while
a large programme of rebuilding the older Holmes 4-4-0s
and 0-6-0s had been practically completed. The coaching
stock, with its red and yellow lining, was also at its
best. It was generally regarded as Scotland's premier
railway. Reaching north from Berwick-on-Tweed on the
east coast and Carlisle on the west, it found its way to
the big cities - Aberdeen, Glasgow, Perth and Stirling -
as well as far into the West Highlands at Fort William
and Mallaig, and also had a big share of much of the
industrial areas including the Clyde. Further, it had a
monopoly in Fife, then rich in coalfields, whilst on a
small scale the golf traffic to St. Andrews must also
have been worthwhile before the rise of the internal
combustion engine.

II
FOREIGN LINES - THE CALEDONIAN RAILWAY

To anyone brought up on the N.B., the Caledonian was a 'foreign' line. Doubtless those born to the C.R. felt the same about the N.B. - indeed, all the very individualistic Scottish railways shared the same sentiments about their immediate neighbours.

Although on my way to school I passed under the Caledonian Railway's branch lines to Leith and Barnton where they crossed the N.B. just east of Haymarket shed, it was seldom that one saw anything passing over. Likewise, I have limited recollections of early visits to Princes Street station. My first real awareness of the Caledonian was seeing their bright blue engines and lake-and-white coaches flashing past on our annual visits to Aberdeen. We then knew we had passed Kinnaber Junction and were running on a 'foreign' railway, at that time something thrilling. Who would have thought, fifty and more years ago, that Kinnaber's importance would have disappeared after the closure in September 1967 of the Caledonian main line from Perth and Forfar, and the diversion of all their services along the Tay from Perth to Dundee and so over the route of their former rivals?

A fortnight's holiday at Bridge of Allan in April 1916 provided my first intimate contact with the Caledonian Railway, and by this time I was old enough to form some impressions, at least of an engine's appearance, sometimes favourable, sometimes otherwise. There was also some thought for the trains themselves and the different coach designs.

The journey from Inverkeithing was via Dunfermline Lower and Upper stations and Alloa to Causewayhead, a small station nestling below the Wallace Monument on the Abbey Craig. From there we continued by horse tram. These ancient four-wheeled trams, pulled by two horses, ran on a track following the edge of the main road from Stirling to Bridge of Allan. The line was nearing the end of its life and the track, especially at passing points, was in very poor condition and derailments were not infrequent. As all was very leisurely in any case this caused no excitement, and it simply meant attaching the horses to the other end of the car and re-railing

with the aid of ramps. Fortunately the distance to be
covered was only 1½ miles.

In the days before motor cars, Bridge of Allan was a
popular holiday centre, blessed also with health-giving
waters, where people went to stay and enjoy the historically interesting locality and numerous walks. This was
to our advantage as most of the long distance trains
stopped there, and one could look at the engines properly
and, better still, become friendly with the drivers.
Outstanding and rostered for the most important expresses
were Smith's ex-'River' Class 4-6-0s, built the year
previously by Hawthorn Leslie of Newcastle and only
recently purchased by the Caledonian, owing to their
alleged unsuitability for the line they were intended
for. With their high running plates based on the Urie
H.15 4-6-0s, they were entirely different from anything
hitherto seen in Scotland. Caley blue, with its deep
crimson running plate and tender frames, did full justice
to the symmetrically-shaped locomotive and, with their
large 21" x 28" cylinders, their departure from Bridge of
Allan northward bound was something worth going to see.
Indeed, they were the most powerful passenger engines on
the railway, easily surpassing the famous 'Cardean'
Class. Another new design in evidence was Pickersgill's
superheated 4-4-0, generally similar in dimensions to
McIntosh's superheated IVth Dunalistairs but differing
in appearance, with no smokebox wingplates and a more
stylish shape of chimney. A six-wheeled tender had also
taken the place of the McIntosh bogie style.

Most of the Caledonian engine classes could be seen,
obvious exceptions being the 0-8-0 tender and tank
engines built for heavy work in the industrial areas,
also the Pickersgill 4-6-2Ts, which were only to be found
on the Clyde Coast trains and banking at Beattock.

Eagerly looked for was a daily freight turn headed by
a McIntosh 2-6-0, a rather odd-looking design with inside
cylinders, making a spirited attack on the five-mile
climb to Kinbuck with a minimum gradient of 1 in 88,
assisted in the rear by a Drummond 0-6-0. Oban trains
were entirely in the hands of McIntosh's 55 Class 4-6-0s
with 5' coupled wheels which first appeared in 1902.
Familiar on these trains was a 45' bogie coach by John
Lambie providing first and third compartments, a lavatory, a luggage compartment and, most interesting, a
first class coupe at one end with end windows. I was

taken on a run up to Dunblane just to sample the novelty
of looking through these windows - only to be rewarded by
a close-up view of the end of the following carriage!
The Highland was another railway that favoured these
strange coupe-end carriages, in their case small four-
wheelers. Early locomotive history was represented by
Brittain's 'Oban Bogie' 4-4-0s of 1882, also assisting
as banking engines. All in all, we had some happy times
at Bridge of Allan station which, alas, no longer exists.
     Apart from passing through the station as a young
child going to and from holidays in the Highlands, my
first proper contact with Perth was in 1919 when, towards
the end of the summer, my brother Douglas and I spent a
day there. The main objective of this visit was to see
one of the new Highland 'Clans' and also to discover
Pickersgill's new 60 Class 4-6-0.
     In addition to being an important centre on the
Caledonian main line and the West Coast Route from Euston
to Scotland, and also the junction for their branch to
Dundee, it was the southern terminus of the Highland
Railway. From the North British came trains from Edinburgh via the Forth Bridge, from Glasgow via Alloa and
the Devon Valley Line and Kinross, as well as locals
along the north shores of Fife and Ladybank. It was one
of those more exalted stations where one could see the
engine and carriage liveries of three different
companies.
     It was essentially a Caledonian station, very apparent
from its appearance and excellent facilities, although
the ownership was shared by the three railways under the
management of the Perth General Station Joint Committee,
consequently being known as Perth General station. The
approach lines were entirely Caledonian, the N.B. coming
in two miles to the south at Hilton Junction, the
Highland seven miles to the north at Stanley Junction.
Undoubtedly the most interesting aspect of Perth General
was the marshalling of the through carriages to or from
Inverness and Edinburgh and Glasgow, which gave the three
shunting tanks a very busy time during rush periods.
These occurred during the early hours, around noon, mid-
afternoon and in the late evenings when the sleepers to
Euston and Kings Cross passed through. Between these
periods the station was quiet except for a fairly
frequent local service to Dundee, 21 miles distant, along
the agricultural plain called the Carse of Gowrie lying

between the southern slopes of the Sidlaw Hills and the
Firth of Tay - these trains being invariably hauled by
McIntosh 0-4-4Ts. There were also freight trains which
passed by outside the main station walls to the marshalling yards lying to the north and south. Each of the
railways supplied their own shunters, those at the time
of this particular visit being a C.R. Drummond 0-4-4T
(No.1230) with solid bogie wheels, built in 1882; a
N.B. 0-6-0T (No.1330), often described as the 'enlarged'
Brighton Terrier, by the same designer in 1877; and
completing the trio was our favourite, Highland No.50B.
This was a little 4-4-0T with Allan 'Crewe'-type framing,
built by David Jones in 1879 and part of the Perth scene
for many years. One would have thought that after the
Grouping Lochgorm would have handed over responsibilities
for shunting the Highland side of the station to
St. Rollox, but No.50B as No.15012 soldiered on until
1929, when it was finally withdrawn.

We were not disappointed with this first visit to
Perth. The 10.05 a.m. from Waverley which we joined at
Dunfermline Lower was a short train, comprising four N.B.
bogie compartment coaches and two Highland non-vestibuled
corridors, hauled by superheated 'Scott' No.417 'Cuddie
Headdrig'. Immediately on arrival we hastened to the
north end of the station to be rewarded by the sight of
No.65, one of Pickersgill's five new 60 Class 4-6-0s,
which had brought in the forenoon express from Buchanan
Street, also with through portions for the Highland.
This was a most graceful-looking engine, especially as it
had outside cylinders - a welcome change for the Caledonian which, continuing the Drummond tradition, had
remained faithful to inside cylinders for many years.
Very smartly the Inverness coaches from Edinburgh and
Glasgow were sorted out, those for the direct line via
Carr Bridge going forward on the 11.50 a.m. express with
its first stop at Blair Atholl. The Forres portions were
attached to the noon train in an adjoining platform.
This was more in the nature of a semi-fast, making calls
at Dunkeld and Pitlochry.

Our main interest now was to see what was going to
take out the 11.50 a.m. and, standing at the ticket
platform at the north end we could see a high-sided
tender, which we knew meant a 'Clan'. No.52 'Clan Munro'
slowly came into full view, and I will always remember
the high tender with its bright red buffer beam and the

steeply rounded cab, extending well beyond the tender
front plate. Viewed from platform level, first impressions were mixed. The general outline had all the
characteristics of a big engine, which it appeared to be
from the official photograph, the only one then available
- but we had not realised that the 'Clan' was in fact
quite small. Emphasising this was the bulky casing along
the running plate concealing much of the Walschaerts
valve gear, which tended to dwarf the comparatively small
boiler: 5' external diameter. With a weight of 62 tons,
the 'Clan' was barely five tons heavier than a superheated 'Dunalistair' or 'Scott'. However, our ideas
changed later in the day when we saw two more 'Clans' and
were able to view them from rail level, for they were
powerful-looking engines.

The noon departure for Inverness via Forres and Nairn
was headed by No.50 'Brodie Castle', and following along
behind a slow for Blair Atholl was one of the old Jones
Strath 4-4-0s, No.99 'Glentromie'.

We saw a lot of engines at Perth that day, including
one of the famous 'Cardean' Class, No.905, which was
stationed there, but generally the Caledonian main line
trains were hauled by McIntosh and Pickersgill superheated 4-4-0s, singly or in pairs.

Among other visits to Perth, one in September 1921
gave me my first view of one of Pickersgill's four new
three-cylinder 4-6-0s. I was standing at the north end
of the main departure platform admiring the latest N.B.
Atlantic, No.510 'The Lord Provost', which had just
placed the through coach from Edinburgh on the 3.50 p.m.
to Inverness, and was idly comparing it with No.50
'Brodie Castle', standing nearby waiting to take the
train out after the connection from Buchanan Street
arrived. To my great surprise this arrived behind
No.956, the first of the class and the heaviest engines
ever built by St. Rollox. Painted shop grey and lined in
black with white edging, it was also fitted with an
indicator shelter. The last engine of the four, No.959,
was stationed at Perth running between there and Glasgow,
and I was able to photograph her several times before all
four engines were found unsuitable for express passenger
work and were sent south to work heavy freight trains
between Carlisle and the Glasgow area.

Perth, always one of my favourite railway haunts, has
seen many changes, due initially to the closure of the

No.770, the last of the N.B. Holmes 729 Class 4-4-0s, at Dunfermline Upper shed in September 1922 shortly after rebuilding. With 24 years active service ahead, she was renumbered 2074 in 1946 and withdrawn in March of that year.

'Auld Reekie', Reid Atlantic No.872, derailed and lying in the sand at Burntisland links on 14 August 1914, surrounded by coal from her tender, which very tragically had enveloped the cab. The crumpled buffer beam was the only contact with the goods train engine.   (Authors Collection)

A summer evening in L.N.E.R. days with a Stirling - Edinburgh local
leaving the Jamestown Viaduct on the 1 in 70 climb to the Forth Bridge,
hauled by non-superheated 'Scott' No.9897 'Red Gauntlet'.

A North British corridor fitted experimentally with a new teak body
conforming to L.N.E.R. standards on new frames carried on the original
bogies. No.32109, the only one of its kind, was photographed at Dalmeny
in the 1950s in British Railways crimson and cream.

Official photograph of No.1239, one of the two N.B.R. steel kitchen-third dining carriages. With a very ample kitchen for those days, these, with a weight of 48tons 10cwts, were the heaviest of the series.

(A.G. Ellis Collection)

Caledonian McIntosh 'Oban Bogie' No.53 at Stirling in 1922. The slip coupling lying on the buffer beam shows that even the premier class on the Oban line took their turn on banking duties on the long bank through Bridge of Allan to Dunblane.

A well-loved Caledonian class, known later as 'Jumbos', was the Drummond 0-6-0, originating in 1883 and finally totalling 244 engines. No.763, photographed at Stirling in June 1926, was one of those painted blue primarily for passenger work.

A unique photograph of a L.S.W.R. Adams 4-4-2T at Blair Atholl in August 1921. The number is unknown, but it has been reported that Nos.0480/1/5/7 of this class had First War service on the Highland. As related in the text, it is very fortunate that this photograph was ever taken.

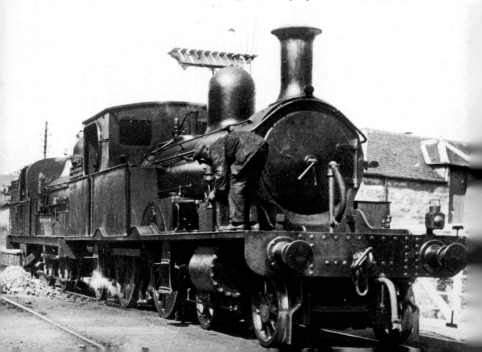

The figure walking so intently towards the engine is the signalman, with the tablet for the waiting fireman. No.99 'Glentromie', a Highland 'Strath', is shown leaving Pitlochry with a northbound 'Blair Slow'.

A memorable day at Kittybrewster shed in September 1921. 1866-built Great North Cowan 4-4-0 No.48A, with its beautifully polished dome and brass work, still to be seen running on the main line out of Aberdeen Joint station.

Whitelegg's swan-song for the Glasgow South Western Railway was his 'Baltic' 4-6-4T Class Nos.540-5. The planished steel cladding on the boiler and cylinders shows fairly well on orthochromatic film in this photograph of No.543 standing at St. Enoch station in the summer of 1922.

A Manson 0-4-4T of 1893 after modernisation by Whitelegg, including larger coal bunker and shorter funnel. No.15253 is shown at St. Enoch on shunting duties in 1926.

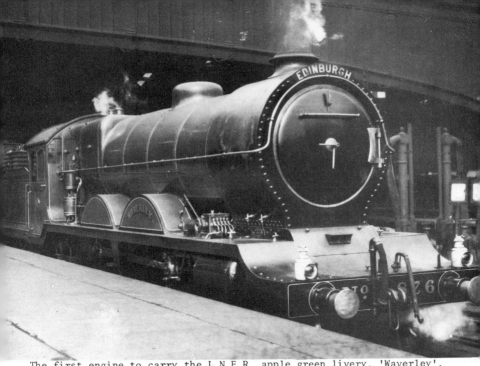

The first engine to carry the L.N.E.R. apple green livery, 'Waverley', still No.876, photographed on the 10.05 a.m. St. Pancras express at Number One platform, Waverley. Note the N.B. lettering and number on the buffer beam; also the brightly polished snap-head rivets on the smokebox.

There was just time to prop my cycle against the footbridge at Causeway-head station and dash over to the other side to get this photograph of Drummond 4-4-0T No.1404, already on the move - evident from the leaking cylinder gland. The train was a Stirling - Devon Valley local.

An imposing view of Atlantic No.9878 'Hazeldean' standing at Inverkeithing on an Edinburgh - Aberdeen express - probably one of the few photographs of this engine in N.B. livery carrying its number in the 9000 scheme.

Rebuilt Holmes 0-6-0 No.663 at Eastfield shed in 1921. With a most substantial tender cab, this engine was for long associated with the West Highland line on engineers' ballast and work trains.

Caley main line to the north via Forfar in 1967 and the
diversion of the Glasgow - Aberdeen trains to Dundee,
there to join the East Coast Route from Waverley. The
sharply curved platforms, previously used by Dundee
trains only, have assumed a new importance and the
booking office, refreshment rooms, etc., have been
transferred to this area, now the only entrance to the
station. The carriageway entrance from the Glasgow Road
Bridge at the north end and the flight of steps at
Craigie Bridge at the south end are no longer available
for public use. More through complete trains between
Inverness and Glasgow and Edinburgh have reduced the
number of through portions and the complicated shunting
operations of the past; consequently, the layout has
been considerably modified and the area of the large
overall roof reduced. Fortunately for those who like the
past, Perth General has merely been pruned and not
rebuilt, so retaining much of its former character and
atmosphere.

Princes Street, Edinburgh, was also frequently
visited in the last days of the Caledonian. In addition
to a regular service to Glasgow, composed of six-wheeled
bogie stock 68½' in length and probably the largest
compartment coaches in the country, other important
trains were to Liverpool, Manchester, and Birmingham,
which were generally attached at Carstairs Junction to
the main train from Glasgow (Central). In some cases the
main train was from Edinburgh, absorbing a Glasgow portion at Carstairs. Invariably these were hauled by
'Dunalistairs' of the earlier second and third classes.

In complete contrast were the small four-wheeled
coaches designed by Pickersgill and built by R.Y.
Pickering in 1922 for the Edinburgh suburban services,
primarily with the very sharp curvature of the Balerno
branch in mind. At first thought it would appear a
little out of place to consider building four-wheeled
coaches at such a late date, but there was a saving in
capital cost and obviously in maintenance. The firsts
and thirds weighed 13½ tons and were 28' 10" in length,
while the van composites were slightly longer and
heavier. All were 9' in width and built to thoroughly
modern standards with the same cross-section of body and
degree of comfort in the compartments as contemporary
bogie stock. These trains were always in charge of
McIntosh's class of twelve 0-4-4Ts built in 1899 with

4' 6" drivers for the Cathcart Circle and the Balerno
lines, both of which had closely spaced stations calling
for quick powers of acceleration.

In Glasgow Central station was quite unsuitable for
photography, although I made a few attempts at time
exposures under the roof and succeeded in getting a
photograph of McIntosh's 30 Class mixed traffic 0-6-0s;
quite a scoop, as there were only four of these, all
employed on the Glasgow Clyde Coast services at that
time.

Finally, there was Buchanan Street, a small station of
only five platforms with no architectural claims of any
sort. The roofing consisted of two longitudinal
sections of gable design supported by rows of pillars,
rather on the lines of the old Euston but considerably
more humble in conception. Buchanan Street dealt with
the Glasgow/Perth - Dundee and Aberdeen traffic as well
as Oban and, of course, Inverness. It was quite busy in
the 1920s but, naturally, many of the engines observed
could also be seen in Perth. Interestingly, in addition
to the normal traffic of the day there were also transfer
services between Buchanan Street and Central - in one
case a train with parcels, taking thirty minutes for the
inter-station journey. In the other direction, there was
a daily fish train and a parcel train which brought in a
Pullman restaurant car for Aberdeen, its inward working
having been to Central. Princes Street and Buchanan
Street are two more stations which have gone, trains to
and from the former having been diverted into the Waverley, which has proved a great improvement for the
interchange of passengers. In Glasgow all traffic for
the north leaves from the one time North British Queen
Street.

The Caledonian was a railway of many locomotive
classes, these in December 1921 comprising:

Tender:			Tank:		
	57	4-6-0		12	4-6-2
	168	4-4-0		12	4-4-0
	5	2-6-0		6	0-8-0
	8	0-8-0		203	0-6-0
	388	0-6-0		135	0-4-4
	29	0-4-2		2	0-4-2
				42	0-4-0

A total of 1,067 engines overall. (The famous Caley
'single' No.123 was not listed as stock at that time.)

With thirteen more wheel arrangements than the North
British, the variety was even greater. Unlike most
British railways (the Great Central being a possible
exception), the authorities at St. Rollox appeared unable
to decide what it really wanted. Perhaps they were
seeking perfection; events proved that they were not
very successful. McIntosh built six different classes of
4-6-0 totalling only 42 in number, most of which were
mixed traffic or express goods with driving wheels of
5' 9" or less. The two Sir James Thompson 4-6-0s of
1903, then the most powerful express engines in Britain,
followed by the five 'Cardeans' of 1906 with 6' 6"
drivers, were very definitely express engines and as such
they distinguished themselves in their early days on the
English traffic over Beattock. Pickersgill produced six
of his 60 Class 4-6-0s, plus his four massive three-
cylinder engines, Nos.956-9, which with 6' 1" wheels were
intended for express work, and lastly his eight little
4-6-0s with 5' 6" wheels for the Oban line.
    With the six 'Rivers' with 6' driving wheels purchased
from the Highland, which for some reason or other were
relegated to express goods work after early successes on
Aberdeen expresses, there were finally 65 4-6-0s on the
Caledonian system (No.907, the last of the 'Cardean'
Class, having succumbed in the Quintinshill disaster of
1915). Comprising ten different classes, mostly mixed
traffic at the best, it was in the event the 4-4-0s that
handled the bulk of the main line trains. Whatever the
merits of the performance of this varied collection of
4-6-0s they all did good work according to the standards
of the day, and were interesting and pleasant-looking
engines to seek out and photograph.
    Railway historians have frequently written about the
famous twelve-wheeled corridors built at St. Rollox in
1906 for the Glasgow/Edinburgh - Aberdeen train known as
the 'Grampian Corridor Express'. A contemporary photograph shows that, initially, these bore painted above the
windows the legend 'Corridor Express Glasgow Perth and
Aberdeen' - Edinburgh being substituted for Glasgow on
the portion from the Capital City. They were still very
much to the fore in the 1920s but were being displaced by
a shorter eight-wheeled corridor by Pickersgill, and it
is two of these which have been so beautifully preserved
by the Scottish Railway Preservation Society.
    The coach livery has often been described as lake-and-

white, but as I recall this it was more of a very dark
plum below waist level rather than lake. This was
carried up to the mouldings around the white panels with
excellent effect. A Caledonian express with its bright
blue engine and attractive train was a magnificent sight,
although not always as sparkling clean as displayed in
their station posters - inevitable in view of the light
colour shades involved. Some of the older stock, particularly the block sets on the Cathcart Circle and other
areas in Glasgow as well as the Barnton and Leith
branches, were - very wisely - painted all over in the
darker colour.

The Caledonian adopted Pullman restaurant cars in
place of dining carriages, the first of these (ten in
number) being built by Cravens in 1914. The choice of
names were those of women famous in Scottish history,
examples being 'Flora MacDonald', 'Fair Maid of Perth'
and 'Lass o' Gowrie'. For the Oban line there was a
Pullman observation car aptly named 'Maid of Morven'.
It is interesting to compare with such names as 'Phyllis'
and 'Rosalind' to be seen farther south.

Memories of the Caledonian would not be complete
without some reference to their stations. While some of
the wayside ones could only be described as ordinary, the
company excelled in their more important centres,
adopting very handsome styles of architecture. Ideal
examples, in addition to Glasgow (Central) and Edinburgh
(Princes Street), were Stirling, Aberdeen Joint, Wemyss
Bay and Gleneagles. During the summer well-kept flower
baskets were suspended from the roof and, on a visit to
the Highland in July this year, it was nice to see Stirling station festooned in similar manner, in addition to
numerous pot plants around the circulating area. It was
the same in Oban.

All in all the Caledonian was a fine railway, and
while not the largest in Scotland generally speaking
offered the best travelling conditions for its
passengers.

III

FOREIGN LINES - THE HIGHLAND RAILWAY

Throughout its existence 'The Highland Railway via Dunkeld' was the heading on one of the station posters of this proud railway, which extended from Perth to Inverness and the lands beyond known as the 'Farther North'. At the Kyle of Lochalsh it was barely a stone's throw away from the Isle of Skye. At first sight the meaning of the wording on the poster appears obscure, but it had a practical purpose, namely to discourage anyone foolish enough to think of travelling to Inverness via Aberdeen and Keith over North British and Great North of Scotland metals. The latter company had long had designs on Inverness with a direct line of their own, but these dreams were finally quashed by the Highland's preparations around 1854 for a direct line across the Grampians to Perth. It is ironical that only last winter, during exceptionally heavy snowstorms, the 'Clansman' from Euston could not proceed beyond Aviemore, 34 miles from its destination, and had to return to Perth and thence via Dundee and Aberdeen - the former Great North route being the only one reasonably clear of snow in the North of Scotland. One wonders if such an arrangement, involving three different companies, would have been practicable in pre-Nationalisation days, and if so how long they would have taken to negotiate.

The Highland was one of my favourites, to some extent because it was associated with holidays, and partly because it traversed very lovely scenery. The drivers, in fact everyone on the railway, were very friendly, and finally there was a great liking for the named engines which came to be regarded by me almost as personal friends. Being a single line with passing places, sometimes entailing long waits for trains, one could feast the eyes on engines at such times and even be invited into their cabs.

Strangely enough the first Highland engines I ever saw were at Inverkeithing, these being en route to or from Hawthorn Leslie's works at Newcastle where many were rebuilt or repaired. This was during the Great War and some time after, Lochgorm Works being quite unable to cope alone with the wear and tear sustained by their engines - many of them aged - due to the heavy naval traffic in both

coal and personnel to Thurso bound for Scapa Flow.
     One of the first attractions of a Highland engine was
the bright green applied as an economy measure even to
the buffer beams at that time, which contrasted boldly
with the N.B. subdued livery. It is interesting to
recall that another war economy was to paint the boilers
black, although the remainder of the engine was green;
also, replacing brass number plates with numbers painted
high on the cab side. This style of numbering appears
on a works official photograph of No.70 'River Ness'
which has been published from time to time. Other
engines that passed by Inverkeithing were Cumming's
heavy goods 4-6-0s, the 'Clans', and 4-4-0s 'Durn' and
'Snaigow'. Several times I saw a 'Clan' waiting in a
loop at Dalmeny on my way home from school.
     It was not until 1921 on an August holiday at
Pitlochry that I first experienced the Highland Railway
on its own territory. Pitlochry was, and remains, a
nice station, and while the buildings on the up side
have been slightly modernised they remain much as I
first saw them over fifty years ago. The station staff
still point out the recess in the stone wall, the
resting place of the large brass bell which was always
rung on the approach of a stopping train. The charming
wooden waiting room on the down side and the little
wooden signal box appear to me at any rate to remain
exactly as they have been since they were built. The
platforms were lengthened with wooden extensions during
the 1914-18 war to accommodate hospital trains bringing
wounded soldiers for treatment and convalescence in
various large local holiday hotels which had been suitably adapted. A nice Highland background to the station
was provided by the sharp peak of Ben-y-Vrackie, but
unfortunately as I soon discovered Pitlochry was a poor
place for photography.
     The train timings naturally corresponded with those
at Perth already described in these pages, but few
except the all station trains between Perth and Blair
Atholl - the 'Blair Slows' - stopped and, in one way or
another, what with position of sun, meal times, etc.,
the net result was only two southbound and three northbound trains suitable photographically and within the
limits of my camera. Obviously I had to go farther
afield and discover Blair Atholl.
     My first trip to Blair was by a forenoon slow hauled

by 'Strath' Class No.97 'Glenmore', built in 1892, and it
was on this train that I experienced the greatest railway
surprise of my life. Approaching any passing place it
was customary to lower the window on the off side to see
what might be waiting for us to get out of the way; and
on this occasion entering Blair Atholl it turned out to
be a London & South Western Railway Adams 4-4-2T leading
yet another surprise, a North Eastern Fletcher 0-4-4T. I
think I had known vaguely that such engines were among
others which had helped out on the Highland during the
war years but had no reason to think they would still be
there. Our train ran right to the north end of the very
long platform, which will be seen from the photograph,
and there was a frantic rush to the south end to photograph the two engines standing there in bright sunlight.
They already had a clear signal. Fortunately the driver
of the Adams had not finished with his oilcan and I was
able to get two photographs, in the case of the leading
not very straight (due to general stress), but I think
these are the only pictorial records of these two engines
in the Highlands, which they were leaving for the last
time.

   Other engines at Blair on that occasion were four of
Peter Drummond's large 0-6-4Ts employed on banking duties
to Druimochdar Summit, and another 'Strath', No.99
'Glentromie'. Finally, most interesting of all, there
was old Clyde bogie No.82, built in 1888. This was name-
less, its name 'Durn' having been transferred to
Cumming's new 4-4-0 in 1916. It was customary at that
time to put the assisting engine on the front of
passenger trains, and it was for such duties that 'Durn'
was primarily at Blair Atholl.

   The 'Straths' were for use on the Blair - Perth slows.
Unfortunately rain set in putting an end to photography,
and as things turned out the two English tanks and three
other photographs taken at Pitlochry were all that I had
to show for this two-week stay on the Highland. What
with camera, film, weather and location, engine photographs did not come easily in those far-off days.

   In August 1922 we had another two weeks at Pitlochry
with more success, especially at Blair Atholl where the
sun shone on the day of my visit. The usual 0-6-4Ts were
in force as well as No.123 'Loch-an-Dorb' and No.1
'Ben-y-Gloe'. Both 'Straths' of the previous year had
gone and replacing 'Durn' was another of the same class,

No.76A 'Bruce', with quite a new coat of green. Another
newcomer was 'Strath' No.100 'Glenbruar', only a few
months returned from a visit to Newcastle, where it had
received a new boiler. It too was looking very smart
after a repaint. Later in the day it made a nice photograph acting as pilot to No.58 'Darnaway Castle', leaving
on the 3.50 p.m. ex-Perth.

Waiting to follow up the hill on a goods train was
Jones 4-6-0 No.103 - now preserved in Glasgow Transport
Museum - and preparing to bank it 0-6-4T No.66. Its
driver had been most helpful shifting engines into
suitable positions for the camera and I was delighted
when he suggested a 'run up the hill' with him. It was
my first footplate run of any length on the Highland and
it took a long time plodding up the fifteen miles to the
summit where, after a final extra push, we dropped
behind. On the way home we stopped exactly opposite
Struan signal box, which was on the up side; and after a
quiet talk with the signalman who was standing on his
tablet-catching balcony, our driver was handed a bottle
of Scotland's Best. Naturally, it went straight to his
locker, but I can remember being extremely worried in
case this was discovered by someone in authority and that
in one way or other I might become implicated. There
were, and likely still are, such happenings in the land
where the peat-flavoured burns flow.

This holiday on the Highland produced quite a good
selection of photographs, assisted by at last finding a
shop which did quite good quality developing and
printing.

Blair Atholl was an important railway centre in those
days. With very few exceptions it was the first stopping
point for long distance northbound trains from Perth, and
the last for southbound. Intermediate passengers used
the 'Blair Slows' which suitably connected the through
trains with Stanley Junction, Murthly, Dunkeld, Dalguise,
Guay, Pitlochry and Killiecrankie. Of these only Dunkeld
and Pitlochry remain. All engines of course took water,
either after or in anticipation of the hard work they
were doing, and to hasten this process of watering twin
water towers were sited at each end of the station. The
line was double-tracked to Dalwhinnie, 23 miles to the
north; in addition to facilitating train movements this
helped to dispose quickly of assisting engines returning
to base. During the Beeching economy years the line was

singled: once again it now enjoys double track, due to
heavy extra traffic concerned with North Sea oil. Blair
Atholl's railway importance continued until the diesel
era, which finally did away with all pilots to the
summit, the station closures disposing of the once-loved
'Blair Slows'.

The Highland locomotive stock in December 1921
totalled 173 engines, comprising:

Tender:	50	4-6-0	Tank:	8	0-6-4
	80	4-4-0		6	0-6-0
	3	2-4-0		5	0-4-4
	12	0-6-0		8	4-4-0
				1	2-4-0

The solitary 2-4-0 tank was a very small machine with
outside cylinders, with the number 118. It was named
'Gordon Castle' after it was purchased from the Duke of
Sutherland, who replaced it with his better-known 0-4-4
tank 'Dunrobin'. This latter is now in a museum on the
other side of the Atlantic after several years on static
display on the Romney Hythe & Dymchurch Railway. On its
purchase by Lochgorm in 1895 the little 2-4-0T was sent
to Sharp Stewart & Co. in Glasgow for rebuilding. Withdrawn in 1923, its last recorded active work appears to
have been shunting at the naval base at Invergordon
during the Great War.

Of the grand total of 173 engines about 99 had names
- one can only give an approximate figure as the ageing
'Duke' Class was being steadily reduced in number. The
'Clans', 'Castles', 'Bens', 'Lochs', 'Straths' and
'Glens' probably made up the best complete set of engine
names chosen by any British railway, representing as
they did the romantic and beautiful country served by
the company. It was always a delight to see one for the
first time, although the same could be said of the 75 or
so goods engines and tanks which had only numbers. I
suppose this was due to the very small engine 'family'
belonging to one railway and the desire to meet each·
member of it. My first introduction to Cumming's 'Durn'
at Perth in 1922 was somewhat dramatic. I had cycled the
32 miles from home to meet my brother who, having a railway servant's all-station pass, had travelled by train.
One of our favourite observation points was the ticket
platform opposite the Highland shed. 'Snaigow' and
'Durn' had always worked between Inverness and Wick

hitherto and we were staggered when the latter suddenly
emerged from the shed. Whether it was this or the long
hard cycle run after a too-hasty breakfast, I don't know,
but I promptly passed out - only for a few seconds,
fortunately. The next mishap was discovering at the
booking office that most of my cash had disappeared - but
this was recovered intact on the ground under the open
wooden decking of the platform. The idea was to train to
Dunfermline Lower and then cycle the last two miles home,
as if nothing untoward had occurred, but it was my
unlucky day. At Dunfermline Lower I tried to walk under
the island platform station name board, which was lower
than I was, and so had to continue by train, reaching
home slightly indisposed. Fortunately, no parental ban
was placed on further cycle runs to Perth.

   The green livery adopted for both engines and carriages could best be described as grass green, with
letter and names in gilt shaded in a lighter green. The
absence of lining was unusual in those days. The small
pattern of Stroudley number plate with wax-filled
counter-sunk numbers on a red background was gradually
being replaced by very large style plates with raised
brass letters and the words 'Highland Railway' in bold
letters, which provided some relief to an otherwise
rather plain-looking turnout by contemporary standards.
'Clans' and 'Castles' also carried the company's crest.
The green applied by Hawthorn Leslie had a very definite
yellow tinge, possibly influenced by the near-at-hand
North Eastern green. This is quite evident even on a
black-and-white photograph on orthochromatic film.

   In the Highland's last days most of the passenger and
goods tender engines could be seen in the south, exceptions being the 'Big Ben' Class which were finally wedded
to Inverness and the North. Interesting also was No.53
'Clan Stewart' which, during the coal strike of 1921 and
subsequent period of fuel shortage was fitted for oil
burning on the 'Scarab' system, the only outward signs
of this being oil tanks on the tender and, not infre-
quently, evil-smelling clouds of smoke due to badly
controlled combustion. Perhaps my greatest favourites
were the 'Straths' which until 1921 were regular visitors
on Perth slows. The following year 'Glenbruar', assisting trains from Blair Atholl, was the last I was to see
south of Aviemore - as in 1923 the family holiday was at
Fort William, and that was the year of sad changes when

approximately twelve of the 'Duke' Class and five of the
'Straths' were withdrawn; a combination of old age and
forward planning by the newly formed London, Midland &
Scottish Railway.

Common to all the Jones designs was the louvred chimney. In a copy of the 'Locomotive' dated March 1903
there appeared an article on locomotive chimneys which,
even at that date, deplored their gradual 'disappearance'
and the consequent increasing inconvenience to Highland
enginemen. Reference was made to relieving this by
providing larger cab windows on the more recent engines
and smoke-deflecting methods, not only on the Continent
but on the engines of the Highland Railway: 'Which were
rendered conspicuous by the arrangement of chimney by
the Late Superintendent David Jones, whose object was to
save the beautiful views on his railway for the tourist
passenger's enjoyment'. I heard no opinions expressed
by drivers on the merits or otherwise of the louvred
chimney, which was really a double casing, with air
entering the louvres and escaping between the outer
casing and the lining - and, it is hoped, carrying the
smoke well above the boiler top.

The Highland had a heterogeneous collection of
carriages, internal corridors with lavatory facilities
predominating on the express trains. Having no restaurant cars vestibuled gangways were not necessary, but
these were being fitted to the final design of coach
with fairly high arced roof and narrow vertical panels
on the sides to enable through passengers to use the
Caledonian Pullman cars south of Perth. On their own
railway the breakfast and lunch baskets supplied at
Perth and, I believe, Aviemore were apparently regarded
as classics of good food and service, tending to be the
privilege of the few and in great demand during the
grouse shooting season.

There was an important innovation in 1922 with the
introduction of Pullman restaurant cars running through
to Aviemore, for which Lochgorm had to collect their
limited number of gangwayed stock together to form into
block sets. On a day when it was the Highland's turn to
supply the through coaches from the south the result was
a symmetrical and bonnie green train with a 'Clan' at
the head and the white-and-umber Pullman in the centre.

Aviemore was a good staging post; for example, the
down breakfast car attached at Perth to the all-night

sleeper from Euston was able to supply lunch on the up
journey, attached to the train leaving Inverness about
11 a.m. for Edinburgh and Glasgow. Similarly, the lunch
cars on the 11.50 a.m. and 12 noon from Perth arrived at
Aviemore in good time to be prepared for attachment to
the evening southbounds for the two Scottish cities and
Euston. The odd man out was the 3.50 p.m. down which
had no restaurant facilities until the North British
decided to put a car on their 2.05 p.m. from Edinburgh,
which had only time to run as far as Blair Atholl before
it was required to return south. Supplying afternoon tea
on the 3.50 p.m. it fulfilled its main purpose, which was
to attract custom to the Inverness - Kings Cross sleeper
on which dinner was available on the fairly long trip
from Blair to Waverley. I recall feeling very proud
watching one of the N.B. ex-E.C.J.S. twelve-wheelers
sailing out on the front of the 3.50 p.m. - these were
the railway operations and train workings which provided
so much pleasure before the railways became less
personal.

Finally, on the subject of rolling stock, were the
fleet of mail vans; the Highland was only a small
railway but the fleet consisted of ten, for Perth to
Wick embraced a large area. Some ran well into British
Railways days and they must have become familiar to
thousands of railway enthusiasts. At the bottom of the
scale were little four-wheeled firsts with coupe ends,
still running between Perth and Blair Atholl.

By December 1922 the Highland Railway had made great
progress after its hard and gruelling period throughout
the 1914-18 war, but there remained the two major problems, heavy gradients and single line working. British
Railways eventually solved the former with diesel power
but the other still remains, and it is not uncommon to
see a sleeping car train for Euston standing for long
periods at Aviemore with the diesel chuffing gently to
itself, awaiting the arrival of a train from the south
which may already have been involved in similar difficulties.

On a visit to Perth General this year I observed how
the two dock platforms at the north end, reserved for
Inverness and Blair Atholl trains, had been filled in for
use as a parcels sorting area. The more elderly will
remember that it was there that they frequently got their
first glimpse of things that were Highland - a guards van

and three coaches all painted in plain green - the
nucleus of the 11.50 a.m. to Inverness, waiting for its
through portions from the south.

IV
FOREIGN LINES - GREAT NORTH OF SCOTLAND RAILWAY

Ballater on Deeside had always been a favourite family
holiday centre of ours, chiefly because my parents hailed
from Aberdeenshire, and it was there in August 1914 that
I first met the Great North of Scotland Railway. Fortunately, I have retained some very clear memories of these
early days; first and foremost among these was what we
called the 'shunt'.

It was customary for us to meet the late afternoon
train, known as the 'Ballater Express', chiefly to buy
the Aberdeen evening newspaper with the latest news of
the war - then but a few weeks old. Whether it was
driver Thomson on No.23 or driver Lamb on No.103, both
Pickersgill 4-4-0s stationed at Ballater, my brothers
and I were always asked to have a 'shunt', this being a
footplate run from the station bufferstops to a point
well up the line where we reversed into the engine shed.
Many will know that Ballater had an exceptionally long
platform built to accommodate the Royal Train, and these
footplate runs were good value for young boys. Further,
there was the joy of helping to push the turntable to get
the engine 'the right way roun fae Aberdeen'.

Another memorable event in the morning was the arrival
of the Ballater 'goods' behind No.18, one of Manson's
4-4-0s - rather a novelty on Deeside with its clumsy
built-up funnel after the Stirling fashion and wide-
spread wingplates, so different from the slim-waisted
Johnson-Pickersgill engines. No.18 also had one of those
peculiar tenders carried on four fixed wheels and a four-
wheeled bogie. We spent hours watching No.18 shunting
about getting its train ready for the return journey to
Aberdeen. Particularly fascinating was rope shunting,
now probably unknown to many, which was simply a time-
honoured method of getting a wagon or wagons into a
siding through a facing point. One end of a long wire
rope was attached to the tender coupling hook, the other
end to a hook on the solebar of the first wagon, which
was positioned some distance from the engine. After the
engine, accelerating fairly quickly, had cleared the
facing point, this was quickly switched over by the
shunter, causing the wagons to trundle into the required

siding and where the hand brakes were applied as necessary.

Recently at Boat of Garten I observed a slip-coupling hook on the solebar of an old Great North four-wheeler which is being painstakingly restored by the dedicated people of the Strathspey Railway.

For passengers for Braemar the railway ran a motorbus service, whilst for heavy goods there was a majestic traction engine with the impressive name 'Braes o' Mar' which rumbled along with two four-wheeled trailers. It must have taken a long time to complete the sixteen or so miles from Ballater, generally uphill, to Braemar standing at 1,100' above sea level, moreover on a water-bound road. A Foden steam wagon with trailer took care of lighter freight.

The railway from Aberdeen to Ballater was constructed over a long period, first on the scene being the Deeside Railway's project: from Ferryhill Junction on the Caledonian Railway, half a mile south of the terminus at Aberdeen, to Banchory - a distance of sixteen miles, completed on 8 September 1853. A further 15½ miles to Aboyne was then undertaken by a company known as the Aboyne Extension and opened on 2 December 1859. A third project optimistically called the Aboyne & Braemar under-took the final section which, due to doubts about the viability of the plan, finally terminated at Ballater, the opening day being 17 October 1866 - a total distance from Aberdeen of 43 miles. The Great North, which all along had powerful interests in the quaintly named little companies, finally absorbed them on 1 August 1875. It was an attractive line, following the Dee for most of the way apart from a detour northwest between Banchory and Aboyne. The outstanding beauty spot was the single plat-form at Cambus o' May, prettily situated among birches by the edge of the river near a very graceful white-painted suspension bridge over the brown slow-moving water. It was still there a few years ago and no doubt will survive for many years more.

In keeping with its long platforms, Ballater had generous station buildings - including a special waiting room reserved for the use of Royalty. Near to the station was a carriage shed which in size greatly exceeded the requirements of the branch, plus a two-road engine shed and turntable.

The premier train in 1914 was the 'Ballater Express',

introduced mainly for Aberdeen businessmen travelling
daily from their summer residences on Deeside. Leaving
Ballater for the city at 8.30 a.m. it called at Aboyne,
Torphins and Banchory, taking 66 minutes for the 43-mile
journey - good going on a line with plenty of hills and
a ruling gradient of 1 in 70 between Aboyne and Banchory.
The down evening train had the same stops at Torphins and
Aboyne but Banchory was served by a slip carriage, an
up-to-date six-wheeled van composite. Obviously introduced as an advertisement, it has a place in railway
history as being the only slip coach ever operated on a
standard gauge single line railway. It only existed for
one season, not being resumed after the war. An all
stations train to and from Aberdeen took approximately an
hour-and-a-half with twelve stops, but omitting the inner
Aberdeen suburban stations which had their own intensive
service through the joint station to Dyce on the main
line to the north. Few trains were seen at Ballater but
the drivers were very friendly, and we spent a lot of
time sitting in their cabs talking to them. The big day
of the month was when the Royal Train arrived, always in
charge of Pickersgill's latests, 4-4-0s with side window
cabs.

The Great War put an end to summer holidays for a
while and six years were to pass before I saw the Great
North again - at Aberdeen in September 1920. I now knew
something about railways and had commenced to use a
camera.

The new joint station started in 1913 had recently
been completed, its construction having been severely
delayed by the war. It was a station typical of the
Caledonian at its best and was jointly owned like its
predecessor with the Great North of Scotland Railway.
Built to cope with any foreseeable increase in traffic it
covered 11½ acres in all, over four of these being roofed
over. With thirteen platforms, the length of the longest
being 1,596' long, it really was a big station.

To link up with the Ballater branch the Great North
had running powers over its partner's lines to Ferryhill
Junction. North British trains were merely guests!

I have vague memories of the old station, which had an
arched roof similar to Queen Street in Glasgow. It was
dark, dingy, had few platforms, and was very cramped.
The platforms were very low and were invariably wet with
dirty water and particles of ice due to fish being

carried by passenger train brake vans, once a common
practice on our railway. Passengers are still reminded
of fish by strong odours from the nearby fish market and
the inevitable flocks of seagulls!

The new station proved very suitable for photography
and I was able to get my first Great North photographs,
also a very fortunate one of an ex-R.O.D. Great Central
Robinson 2-8-0 - then on loan to the Caledonian.
Although taken in poor light this photograph did record
a comparatively brief locomotive operation.

The next visit to the northeast was exactly a year
later in September 1921, with an unforgettable experience
one morning at the Joint when I caught a fleeting glimpse
of a small outside-cylindered 4-4-0 leaving the north end
tender-first, no doubt heading for Kittybrewster shed.
To my utter surprise it had a shining brass dome and
polished copper-capped chimney. I had no idea that such
anachronisms existed in Aberdeenshire, and it was obvious
that Kittybrewster shed had to be discovered. Next
morning I found that a large part of the shed layout was
easily visible from the platform end at Kittybrewster
station. It was very tantalising viewing all the engines
including the antique of yesterday and wondering how to
get there. Fortunately, my father was with me, and he
settled the problem simply by leading the way over the
running lines into the shed and getting permission to
look round. Undoubtedly his clerical collar helped.

Kittybrewster shed, the largest on the system,
supplied motive power for the main line to Elgin and the
various branches to the east coast as well as the Ballater branch. Also stationed there were the nine 0-4-4Ts
for the Aberdeen suburban service, some of the 0-6-0Ts,
and the small shunters employed in the docks. In
addition it was parent to a large number of small branch
line sub-sheds. The two other major sheds were at Keith,
an important interchange point, and Elgin.

Kittybrewster was an excellent place for photography,
not only on the spacious approach lines and sidings but
at the shed itself. Built on the open roundhouse princ-
iple, there was plenty of room to photograph an engine
on the turntable as it turned to a nice sunlit position.
There was no coaling stage, merely a steam crane with a
vertical boiler which hoisted and swung loaded coal
buckets over the tender. A fireman then completed the
operation by banging a catch on the bucket with a heavy

hammer, so releasing the contents. This little crane had
a very busy day.

Another Kittybrewster museum piece was the breakdown
crane. Sturdy-looking, and carried on a compact six-
wheeled truck, it had a lifting capacity of fifteen tons
and was hand-operated.

Fortunately, the sun was shining on this, my first
ever visit to Kittybrewster; and I soon had a nice picture of the engine with the beautiful dome, which turned
out to be No.48A, one of the three old Cowan engines
built in 1866 which were bequeathed to the L.N.E.R. in
1923. The other two were No.44A and No.45A. Another
prize was the outside-cylindered 4-4-0 No.1 which,
together with No.2 and No.3, built in 1878-9, were the
last engines designed by Cowan. Their driving wheels
were 6' 1" in diameter compared with his previous standard of 5' 6½". No.1 had lost all the brass and copper
carried by No.48A when it was rebuilt by Pickersgill in
1897, but the slotted driving splashers were still
apparent although plated over on the inner side.

September 1922 was the occasion of my last contact
with the G.N.S.R., three months before it became part of
the L.N.E.R., and it was at Kittybrewster that I met
No.45A, the most celebrated of the three old Cowan
engines, which was standing in the coal queue having
arrived on a local from Inverurie. She was introduced
to me by the shed people, obviously very proud of her, as
'Meldrum Meg' - a name earned after a long period as
branch engine at Old Meldrum, the terminus of the short
line from Inverurie. Further, they posed her beautifully
on the turntable for a photograph. This delightful old
engine's finest hour was at the Darlington Centenary
Celebrations in 1925 when she took her place with a train
of contemporary four-wheeled coaches in the final proces-
sion of trains. These represented the latest passenger
stock of the L.N.E., L.M.S., Great Western and Southern
Railways and, last of all, 'Locomotion' (with a petrol
engine concealed in her tender), hauling a replica of the
first passenger train in the world.

In December 1922 the G.N.S.R. possessed 122 locomotives, all 4-4-0s with the exception of nine 0-4-4Ts, a
similar number of 0-6-0Ts, and the four 0-4-2Ts built in
1915 by Manning Wardle & Co. for shunting in Aberdeen
docks. There was no class specially assigned to goods
traffic although in earlier days driving wheels varied in

diameter from 5' 6" to 6' 1" with three exceptions -
Manson's final design with 6' 6½" drivers, built in 1890.
Johnson's first engine, built in 1893, had 6' 1" wheels,
which remained standard on the Great North right to the
end, all engines so equipped taking their turn on
passenger and goods trains alike. Nevertheless, the
total of exactly one hundred 4-4-0s were so varied as to
warrant eleven different classifications under the
L.N.E.R. - D.38 to D.48.

The ultimate in express engines was Heywood's superheated 4-4-0, six built by the North British Locomotive
Co. in 1920 and two in 1921 - these latter, very appropriately, constructed at Inverurie. The engine weight
was 48tons 13cwts attached to a comparatively large
tender weighing 37tons 8cwts. All bearing names,
probably the most illustrious being No.49 'Gordon
Highlander', now preserved in ·Glasgow Transport Museum,
they were the last moderate to small-sized passenger
engines built in this country and considered by many to
be the prettiest.

Passenger rolling stock generally was extremely good
after greatly needed improvements by Pickersgill in
1896, two years after he was appointed locomotive and
carriage superintendent. His first design was one of
the earliest corridor coaches in this country. Running
on six wheels, they were 36' in length and equipped with
lavatories. There were no end vestibules, the end seats
occupying the full width of the compartment, a common
enough practice at the time. A tremendous innovation
was the provision of electric lighting, each coach
having its own generator and accumulators - which looked
very uncommon on a non-bogie vehicle. As I remember
Great North coaches they were either lit by oil lamps or
by electricity, there being no transition period of gas.
Two years later in 1898 came the first bogie corridor
carriage with a somewhat low elliptical roof. Provision
was made for flexible gangways if called for in the
future. The ultimate passenger rolling stock, a development of the 1898 pattern with higher roof and lights
above the windows, provided a high standard of
furnishings and comfort. These, with flexible gangways,
could be seen on the through coach service to Waverley,
and like the rest of the railway's rolling stock they
were kept immaculately clean.

Pickersgill was also responsible for a new livery

which continued right through to the Grouping. Often
described as a dark purple lake - I think of it more in
terms of chocolate - it was applied to the lower portion
of the carriage body with cream from just below the
window sills to the roof cantrail. With gold lining and
lettering they were very beautiful indeed. For less
important duties there were non-corridor coaches built to
the same standards, firstly with six wheels and then on
four-wheeled bogies. An interesting feature on the older
passenger brake vans was a dog compartment which had two
outside doors, with ordinary door handles on the vanside
side just above footstep level. There was a lot of dog
traffic at Ballater during the holiday season leading up
to the 'Glorious Twelfth', when these compartments served
a very useful purpose.

The Great North was the only Scottish railway to have
a Royal Train, and the 'Locomotive Magazine' of February
1904 refers to a compliment paid to the company in September of the previous year by H.M. King Edward VII on
holiday at Balmoral, when he 'commanded' its use for a
visit to Rufford Abbey for the Doncaster Race Meeting.
Used throughout the Doncaster week for conveying the
royal party from Ollerton to Doncaster, it also made a
trip to Kings Cross before finally returning to Ballater
via York and the East Coast Route. One photograph shows
a train of two bogie vans, two bogie coaches, the Royal
Saloon and three six-wheelers, none of which were
through-vestibuled. Fortunately, this unique Royal
saloon survived the years and is now in the good care of
the Scottish Railway Preservation Society.

A further activity of this enterprising little railway
was in operating bus services, in which they were
pioneers among railways. They were introduced on the
Braemar route in 1904, apparently with such success as to
warrant the opening of further services in various other
parts of Aberdeenshire. One of these, the Ballater -
Braemar, was taken over by the L.N.E.R. and was running
at least until 1928. The bodies were painted apple green
with L.N.E.R. transfers on a wood-grained surface panel
below the windows, and cream window frames and roof.

The Great North of Scotland was the smallest Scottish
railway, yet paradoxically it was the only one to use the
word 'great' in its title. After early vicissitudes it
developed into one of the best-run railways in this
country, earning towards the end of the last century the

honour of being known as 'Little and Good'. It had a
monopoly of Aberdeenshire north of the River Dee and
nearly all of Banffshire, apart from Highland intrusions
to Keith and a branch to Buckie which joined the Great
North route 'via the coast' between Elgin and Aberdeen.
Elgin was its main line terminus in Morayshire unless one
considers Lossiemouth, the final extremity, 5½ miles
further on.

The Great North as we all knew it was a very smart
railway. Their little 4-4-0s were still in active service into the 1950s, and it is not only the more elderly
who will never forget how rapidly they accelerated away
from a wayside station - or their equally fast arrivals,
for a Great North driver's handling of the Westinghouse
brake was certainly unrivalled. The sound of their
shrill whistles heralding the approach as they passed the
distant signal was a delight; to me it was the distant
signal at Tullich on the final run in to Ballater.

V

FOREIGN LINES - GLASGOW & SOUTH WESTERN RAILWAY

Curiously enough, it was while on holiday at Melksham in Wiltshire in 1916 that I first set eyes on a Glasgow & South Western engine. Some of my friends had told me that if I went to the station I would see a 'Scotch' engine, which I immediately took to be a leg pull. Nevertheless, it turned out to be a G. & S.W.R. Smellie 0-6-0, some of which were on loan to the Great Western, very likely to adjust another loan by Swindon to somewhere else.

Unfortunately, after that first strange encounter, I seldom saw much of Scotland's third largest railway simply because it was well off the beaten track from Inverkeithing. In pre-Grouping days train fares were not very plentiful and unfortunately there were no relatives in Glasgow or nearby, so that cycling was out of the question. Further, the family did not favour holidays in the southwest. In later days with limited free time the tendency was to concentrate on the nearer-at-hand railway centres, relying for greater variety on the annual summer holiday.

Consequently it was not until April 1922 that I first set eyes on the Glasgow & South Western Railway - at St. Enoch, its Glasgow terminus. My aim then was to see and photograph one of Whitelegg's new 4-6-4 tank engines. St. Enoch was nicely placed for the morning sun, there were no ticket collecting barriers, and of great assistance there was a subway connecting each platform sited halfway along their total lengths. By standing on the platform and studying the points it was possible to decide for which train an engine coming from the shed was destined. Some of the trains were very short, so there had to be a rush down the subway steps and up again to try and photograph the engine before it disappeared under the station roof. At the end of the main departure platform there was a convenient set of points, part of a triangle at which engines paused when they were turning. Their stops were necessarily brief, but sometimes the drivers were kind to photographers.

I was able to secure a particularly nice photograph of No.540, the first of the 'Baltics', standing on the

5.10 p.m. to Ayr, one of the railway's prestige trains.
This photograph, published in the 'Locomotive News' of
10 June 1922, was the first of these engines to appear in
the railway press apart from an official one of the
engine in works grey paint supplied by the builders
(North British Locomotive Co.). Shortly after this, on a
cycle run to Stirling in quest of photographs, I remember
stopping at the roadside just to look at this photograph,
and I have often wondered since how many of my contemporaries
did the same sort of thing. After all it was a
very new engine, and this was the first photograph I had
seen of it in active service.

There were six of these 'Baltics' which, carrying a
boiler of 5' 6" in diameter and large cylinders of
22" x 26", turned the scales at 99 tons. They were
magnificent-looking engines in every way, attracting much
attention from the boiler clothing plating which was
finished in what was referred to as 'planished steel'.
As I remember it, this could be described as a stainless
steel with the mirror-like surface muted to a light blue-
grey sheen. It looked very effective allied to the
company's grass green livery, black-and-white lining and
crimson running plate.

Designed for the short routes to the Clyde Coast, six
were distributed between Ayr, Fairlie Pier, and Glasgow
(Corkerhill). One was retained at Hurlford possibly to
facilitate the study of performance when being employed
between Kilmarnock and St. Enoch.

Regrettably the 'Baltics' had many failings, heating
troubles being among them - also a tendency to roll on
imperfect track, not unknown on other companies which had
sponsored the very large tank engine. However, I continued to see these 'Baltics' from time to time and
without exception their drivers were full of praise for
them and completely loyal to their designer.

There was plenty to see at St. Enoch, including
Manson's nice-looking medium-sized 4-6-0s, also Peter
Drummond's large 4-4-0s, at the time of building reported
to be the heaviest engines of this wheel arrangement in
the country.

Also much in evidence were Manson and Smellie 4-4-0s,
rebuilt and generally modernised by Whitelegg under a big
programme which included standardisation of boilers. His
most spectacular rebuild really amounted to a complete
renewal, the subject being four-cylindered 4-4-0 No.11

designed by Manson and at the time of completion in April
1897 the first four-cylindered engine in the United
Kingdom. The reconstruction which took place in 1922
included a boiler of the Drummond superheated 4-4-0 type
and a low funnel not unlike those on the 'Baltic' tanks.
Still retained were the old-fashioned driving wheel
splashers and the wheels. No.11 was named 'Lord Glen-
arthur', the name of the chairman of the company.

At the time of the Grouping the G. & S.W.R. possessed
528 locomotives, comprising:

Tender:	55	0-4-2	Tank:	10	0-4-0
	3	2-4-0		18	0-6-0
	177	0-6-0		20	0-4-4
	181	4-4-0		28	0-6-2
	19	4-6-0		6	4-6-4
	11	2-6-0			

Few of the older engines survived long after 1923.

St. Enoch station was a very fine station indeed, very
similar to St. Pancras and with the same high level
approach, fronted by a large and spectacular hotel. At
its opening in 1876 it had a large single arch. A
smaller one was added in 1901 and there were finally
twelve platforms covering an area of 13½ acres. It was
the headquarters for a railway which served the southwest
of Scotland through the Burns Country to Stranraer as
well as the Clyde Coast, on which it had a large fleet of
steamers competing very earnestly with the Caledonian
Railway. Its main line was via Kilmarnock and Dumfries
to Carlisle, where it joined its close English partner
the Midland. It is interesting to read that at a special
meeting of the G. & S.W.R. shareholders in 1873 a bill
was approved calling for amalgamation with the Midland
Railway - rejected by Parliament later in the year.

Amplifying the Midland atmosphere at St. Enoch was the
company's coach livery. Lined in black and gold, the red
was but a shade lighter than that applied at Derby.
There was also the presence of clerestory-roofed Derby-
built stock on the through trains from St. Pancras.

A single Glasgow & South Western engine remains today,
one of three outside-cylindered side tanks with Walschaerts valve gear built by Drummond in 1917. Sold to
various collieries many years ago the last survivor is
now in Glasgow Transport Museum. Beautifully restored by
the museum staff (with, I believe, a chimney turned on a

lathe from a solid block of wood), it proudly takes its place beside its Caledonian, North British, Highland and Great North of Scotland relatives.

VI
THE GROUPING - 1923

Probably the most interesting item included in the
1922 edition of the 'Railway Year Book' concerned the
formation into four groups of the railways of Great
Britain in accordance with the Railways Act of 1921.
These were referred to in the Schedule of the Act as:

1. Southern Group
2. Western Group
3. North Western, Midland and West Scottish Group
4. North Eastern, Eastern and East Scottish Group

which became known on 1 January 1923 as:

Southern Railway
Great Western Railway
London Midland and Scottish Railway
London and North Eastern Railway

These titles were to remain familiar until Nationalisation came into force on 1 January 1948, a quarter of a
century later.
First impressions were that London & North Eastern was
nicely traditional and that Great Western was ideal for
its area of the country. London Midland & Scottish
sounded rather clumsy, and there was a definite feeling
that there should have been a 'Great' in front of
'Southern' in accordance with past railway customs.
These criticisms, however, were soon forgotten when the
publicity departments of the two railways concerned made
it clear that they wanted their railways to be popularly
known as 'L.M.S.' and the one word 'Southern', these
titles being appropriately stressed on station signs,
posters and other advertising media. Similarly, the
London & North Eastern's earlier L. & N.E.R. was shortened into the neater and more euphonious L.N.E.R., which
again was presented to and accepted by the public as the
popular title for the railway.
We were soon to observe signs of a considerable degree
of competition between the new railways, all of which had
their faithful supporters who were naturally biased
towards their favourite constituent company - mine of
course being the L.N.E.R. with a special regard for the

Southern Scottish Area, formerly the North British
Railway.

The first evidence of the new regime was a poster
displayed in every station showing the name of the new
company in very prominent letters together with those of
the old, and commencing with the words 'Our New Name',
concluding with 'Our Aim to Serve You'. I can recall no
regrets whatsoever about the passing of the North British
Railway; rather was there a keen anticipation of the
future and a feeling of pride that 'our railway' was to
be united with the railway giants of the south, moreover
with a head office in London - sentiments quite inapplic-
able in such a geographically-placed situation arising at
the present time. . . . Particularly satisfying was the
appointment of the North British chairman, William
Whitelaw, to the chairmanship of the new railway; a move
which must have assisted Scottish acceptance of decisions
made in London. I remember several of my driver friends
referring to him as a 'guid man for the job', which
indeed he was, as he brought with him a lot of railway
experience gained not only from the N.B. but also the
Highland - of which he had also been chairman for a
period.

Yes, we enthusiasts had many thoughts about the future
and foremost of these was locomotive policy and other
exciting things like engine and carriage liveries.
Engines we assumed would be green, simply because it was
the colour used in varying shades by a majority of the
constituent companies, and with Sir Nigel Gresley in
charge the first choice appeared to be Great Northern
apple green. It soon leaked out, however, that the
director had already given a lot of thought to this question, as on 31 January 1923 they inspected at York both
passenger and goods engines from the Great Northern,
North Eastern, Great Central as well as a passenger
locomotive from the North British. A significant
absence was a representative from Stratford. All were
painted in their original liveries, but with the lettering L. & N.E.R. and number on tender or tank sides in
the respective pre-Grouping style of transfers. The N.B.
representative was Atlantic No.874 'Dunedin' in bronze
green and lettering, with number in the Cowlairs style of
gilt transfers, which incidentally were extremely attractive. Very noticeable was the inevitable absence of the
N.B. crest on the driving splasher.

Another parade was held at Marylebone on 22 February 1923 when in addition to some of the engines already inspected representatives of the same four railways were displayed in Great Northern green, omitting the traditional Doncaster olive green edging on tenders, etc.; further, the chocolate running plate and tender frames had been changed to black with a neat red line in accordance with North Eastern practice, a happy marriage of the engine liveries of the two most important companies. The N.B. model was another Atlantic, No.876 'Waverley', lettered again in the N.B. style including the stylish buffer beam numerals.

It was now obvious from the nature of the exhibits that Doncaster apple green had already been chosen for the new passenger livery, which it was decided should apply generally to engines with driving wheels exceeding 6' in diameter. Very wisely Cowlairs applied it to their 6' wheeled 'Glens', a tribute to their first-class work on the West Highland and elsewhere on the system. On this second inspection the Great Eastern was represented by a Holden 4-6-0, No.1534, with the full Great Northern treatment including chocolate running plate, etc.

One wonders if serious thought had ever been given to the N.B. bronze green. Obviously there had to be a Scottish representative, and what more appropriate than one of the chairman's own Atlantics?

Goods engines followed former North Eastern practice, black with red lining, which also applied to mixed traffic engines and unfortunately to all tank engines, both passenger and goods. 'Waverley' was the first green N.B. engine I saw when after her Marylebone debut she started work on the Waverley Route, based at Canal shed (Carlisle). Very bonnie she looked, and the general impression was of a much larger engine than hitherto.

As regards passenger coaches the forecast in our part of the country was red, there already being three examples: Great Eastern, North Eastern and North British. No thought whatsoever was given to red appearing on the L.M.S., which would surely adopt something related to the L.N.W.R.-C.R. two-tone liveries. As for varnished teak, that by its very nature appeared quite out of the question on the vast number of painted coaches of the old companies.

Early in the spring I was delighted to see in the Waverley two obviously new North Eastern compartment

coaches of their latest design, painted in their attractive shade of lake with numbers on the doors indicating
first or third class. Obviously, I thought, this was it,
the new L.N.E.R. coach livery, at the same time rather
gratified that N.B. style transfers had been used for the
doors; but these were idle thoughts, as it soon trans-
pired that these carriages, together with others to
follow, were intended to replace aging and uncomfortable
stock on the Edinburgh suburban service.

In May it became known that the L.N.E.R. was going to
adopt varnished teak with the customary East Coast stock
red-and-yellow lining and letter shading, not the blue-
and-yellow of the Great Northern. A suitable shade of
brown paint, with hand-applied simulated wood graining
replacing the pre-1923 liveries, would be adopted. An
earlier example of this finish could of course be seen
on the older rolling stock of the Great Central which at
one time had lake lower and 'french grey' upper panels.

At first the different paint shops' interpretations
of 'varnished teak' differed considerably, but it soon
became uniform and pleasing to the eye. Looking considerably farther ahead, many who remember the 'Flying
Scotsman' with Thompson's post-war design of steel-sided
carriages would agree that it looked every way as good
if not better than the true varnished teak, which did
darken with age and repeated coats of varnish. In their
first efforts Cowlairs, obviously thinking in terms of
the East Coast square-cornered mouldings, applied the
red-and-yellow lining along the centre of these,
completely disregarding the more traditional curved
corners. The result was an unsightly collection of
horizontal and vertical lines crossing each other at
intervals.

Meanwhile engines were being turned out from Cowlairs
in varying garbs. Many appeared in bronze green fully
lined, either lettered N.B. cr L. & N.E.R. The N.B.
crest was of course missing and likewise the brass
number plate, which was replaced by a new standard
smaller one with raised brass number and lettering,
building or rebuilding date on a black background.

No.1162, one of our Wheatley 0-6-0s dating back to
1870, was the first engine to appear at Inverkeithing in
the new goods livery, black with red lining, L. & N.E.R.
and number again in N.B. transfers. The same was
applied to green 'Scott' No.895 'Rob Roy', which was

operating from St. Margaret's shed to Perth and causing
quite a stir there with its gay colour. This temporary
phase soon ended, however, with the introduction of the
well-known L.N.E.R. transfers - gold for passenger with
red and black shading for green engines, and yellow for
goods, with red and brown shading. For some reason or
other Cowlairs initially used brown shading on both green
and black engines, and doubtless many will have noted the
same on the 'Flying Scotsman', now a close neighbour of
mine at Carnforth. Minor points like these may now seem
trivial but they caused a lot of interest at the time,
especially among the younger enthusiasts who at that time
comprised the majority of those who had an affection for
railway locomotives. Another impending change was the
addition of a small 4½" suffix to the engine number
indicating the area of origin. For example, North
British No.868 became 868B while Great North of Scotland
No.72 became 72S. Also to be seen in Edinburgh would be
North Eastern 2207D - that letter signifying Darlington,
'E' having been appropriated by the Great Eastern. No
longer would one see two engines bearing the same number
in the Waverley, for example N.E. Worsdell R 4-4-0 No.592
and N.B. Holmes 7' 4-4-0 bearing the same number - both
engines in apple green.

During the Easter holidays I cycled to Stirling
primarily to see if there were any changes on the London
Midland side, but beyond station notices and poster
boards bearing the letters L.M. & S.R. or the name of the
railway in full there was nothing new. Secrecy still
surrounded Euston's intentions about a new rolling stock
colour scheme but at that time we were quite unaware of
the policy differences that existed between Crewe and
Derby, considering the former to be all powerful. I had
then only seen the Midland Railway twice on brief visits
to Carlisle and engine-wise thought their locomotives
were rather odd and small-looking, with cabs well open to
the weather, somewhat long chimneys, and dust shields
resembling cricket pads ahead of the leading bogie wheels
(provided to protect bearing surfaces at water troughs
from pilot engine tenders) - symbolic of continual
double-heading. Their general run of small tenders also
called for criticism, quite unfounded, as we had forgotten the existence of water troughs south of the border.
Our ideas changed a lot a few years later when Derby
compounds took their place on the Caledonian and Glasgow

& South Western with great distinction.

Stirling station was quite busy that day and it was fortunate that No.192, one of Pickersgill's new 4-6-0s for the Oban line, made its appearance. All in immaculate Caley blue, eight of these engines were delivered just after the formation of the L.M.S. Other engines of note were two of Pickersgill's new 60 4-6-0s and an ex-Highland 'River', also several of McIntosh's 5' wheeled 4-6-0s, again specially built for working to Oban. To complete the picture was one of Brittain's quaint little 'Oban Bogie' 4-4-0s, built in 1882, employed in station shunting - some of which duties I enjoyed in its very meagre cab. I will always remember the rail beats of the little four-wheeled tender trundling along behind this 4-4-0.

The North British had two sheds at Stirling. The more important one on the east side near the banks of the twisting Forth had a fairly large complement of engines for use on the trains to Edinburgh via Alloa and Dunfermline and on the Devon Valley Line via Dollar and Rumbling Bridge to Kinross, both passenger and goods. Rebuilt Holmes 4-4-0s and 0-6-0s were much in evidence as well as two little Drummond 4-4-0Ts - the solid bogie wheeled variety - for use on the branch to Alva at the base of the Ochil Hills. Also present were a few 0-6-2Ts for short trips from the collieries situated eastwards towards Alloa.

Opposite, on the west side of the up and down lines, was a small shed, formerly the property of the Forth & Clyde Railway - a title which accurately described its route from Stirling via Balloch at the foot of Loch Lomond to the shores of the Clyde at Dumbarton. The short distance from Balloch to Dumbarton, jointly owned by the C.R. and N.B., was known as the Dumbarton & Balloch Joint. On shed for working on this line was Drummond 0-4-4T No.1326. Built in 1877, this class of engines were originally 0-4-2Ts. There was also a more modern version by Holmes, 0-4-4T No.591. For goods traffic two rebuilt Holmes 0-6-0s were available. Unfortunately the weather clouded over badly and the only photographic reward on that trip was a photograph of 4-4-0 No.736 and, thanks to a glimmer of sun at Causewayhead on the way home, a lively little picture of Drummond 4-4-0T No.1404 taking off on a Devon Valley train.

Another Easter holiday visit was to Dunfermline Upper

shed. Only a couple of miles from home, it had been
familiar to me for several years; indeed, it was the
first shed I had ever set foot in. The foreman was very
willing to let me come and go as I wished, and everyone
at the shed was helpful about shifting engines to
suitable positions for the camera. Well do I remember
drivers slowly moving their engines, always leaning well
out of their cabs to ensure that the coupling rods were
fully exposed: 'the rods must be doon'. The shed's
primary importance was related to coal, for which it was
well situated to cover the big West Fife coalfield -
eastwards towards Cowdenbeath and Kelty and to the west
in the direction of Alloa. That is but a brief description of a vast coal belt with minor branch lines to the
numerous pits. Rich coalfields once and a source of
great wealth to the North British Railway, they have long
since been worked out - although a few new collieries
have been opened in more modern times - and the sites of
many that have passed on have completely disappeared,
their waste heaps having provided useful material for new
road works, or in some cases landscaped.

It is obvious that Dunfermline Upper was a most
important shed on the North British, and to simplify
identification of a brief summary of the locomotives
stationed there in the earliest days of the Grouping use
has been made of the new L.N.E.R. classification scheme
which was inaugurated some months later in September.

First in importance were the heavy coal trains to
Aberdeen, and for these were two Class J.37 0-6-0s,
No.162 and No.157, and also J.35 No.855. Although these
were capable engines they were not really suited for
heavy mineral traffic, and it is not surprising that the
North British had been organising comparative tests with
a Great Western 2-8-0 and a North Eastern 0-8-0 with
three cylinders, which had resulted in the preparation of
drawings of a three-cylindered 0-8-0 of their own.
Naturally the new leadership at Doncaster had other ideas
about this and in mid-1923 tests were carried out from
Thornton shed using a Great Central 04 2-8-0 and a North
Eastern T.2 0-8-0.

For secondary goods work and local coal traffic,
Dunfermline Upper had about ten of the most versatile
J.36 0-6-0s - Holmes engines rebuilt by Reid with a long
life ahead of them - and for the shorter distances interconnecting the coal pits with Townhill Marshalling Yard a

Derby red comes to the Caledonian; McIntosh 0-4-4T No.15151 in April 1924 at Dalry Road shed, with the island platform station in the background. This was one of a class of tank engines with 4' 6" coupled wheels used on the sharply graded Balerno branch.

Newcomer to the Southern Scottish Area. Former North Eastern 0-6-0 No.1897D (L.N.E.R. J.24) on a northbound coal train passing through Inverkeithing - for Rosyth Dockyard. . . .

The last of the ten 4-6-0s of the 'Sir James King' Class, built in 1906
for express mixed traffic duties, was No.917. Fitted experimentally in
1910 with a side-windowed cab, she is seen here at Perth shed in 1924
painted red and numbered 14618.

By no means a perfect photograph but historically interesting is this
view of two old stagers lying in a siding at Aviemore shed in August
1924 awaiting removal for breaking up. The engines are No.91A
'Strathspey', 1892, and 'Clyde Bogie' No.79A 'Atholl', 1886.

A pictorial record at Dingwall station of the incident referred to in the text of 'Skye Bogie' No.14277 just returned from Lochgorm Works, complete with No.14282's tender.

The forenoon Strathpeffer branch train has just backed on to the through coach from Inverness, an ex-Midland composite matching the guards van on the branch set. The engine is H.R. No.101, one of the two 4-4-0Ts originally built by Dubs & Co. in 1893 for a South American railway.

Photographed a few days after the end of the General Strike in 1926,
rebuilt Holmes 4-4-0 No.9731 is at the head of a Stirling - Edinburgh
train at Inverkeithing. The large sheet on the cab roof was extended over
the tender as stone-throwing was occurring at various points on the line.

Among the large variety of engines available for the camera at the
Stephenson Locomotive Society visit to Stirling on 5 June 1926 was
No.17902, one of five McIntosh express goods engines with large 5' 2¼"
diameter boilers built in 1906.

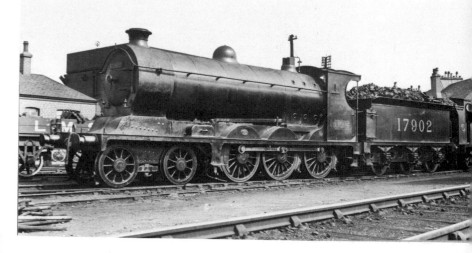

Carstairs, July 1926, with Derby compound No.1066 fitted for oil
burning, standing on the very sharply curved spur from the Edinburgh
line to the main line at Strawfrank Junction.

Heywood 4-4-0 No.6847 'Sir David Stewart' under repair at Kittybrewster
August 1926. .Note the stout wooden prop under the cab; also part of
the engine's bogie. At the time the engine had lost its superheated
boiler, hence the covering on the extended front end, normally
accommodating an extended smokebox.

Causing quite a sensation in the North in 1926 was Fowler 'Jinty' 0-6-0T No.16415, which is seen posing immaculately on the turntable at Inverness shed in front of the historical entrance arch/water tank.

Superheated Manson 4-4-0 No.6877 at Elgin shed in August 1926, all polished up prior to taking over an Inverness - Aberdeen express. Peculiar to this engine were the lined panels on the splashers.

L.N.E.R. Class J.38 0-6-0 No.1414 passing Craigentinny on a train of coal discharged at Leith Docks from the Continent during the prolonged Coal Strike of 1926.

'Scottish Director' No.6397 'The Lady of the Lake' on the turntable at Eastfield beside the shed foreman's office, surmounted by its magnificent clock.

Manson 4-4-0 No.14268 was one of the many subjects photographed on the S.L.S. visit to Kilmarnock Works and Hurlford shed in the summer of 1927.

First photograph of an L.M.S. 'Royal Scot' No.6127 at Murrayfield Junction early on a September morning in 1927. An hour later a successful photograph would have been impossible, as by then the sun would have been shining directly on the lens.

selection of about eight old Drummond Class J.34 0-6-0s,
which included No.30, No.163, No.1297 and No.538. Built
1879-83, they had all been rebuilt prior to 1910. They
were aging, and although we did not realise it at the
time were on the way out. A loner was No.159, a Holmes
17" 0-6-0 Class J.33 which, with other duties, helped out
with banking at Inverkeithing with the Drummonds.
Banking at Inverkeithing was primarily in the hands of
Wheatley 0-6-0s Class J.31, regulars still being No.1162,
No.1122, and No.1223. Although dating back to 1870 they
had received new boilers as recently as 1916 and were in
good fettle, and very capable of handling the hard work
demanded from them. Ten N.15 0-6-2Ts and two J.83
0-6-0Ts provided the power for shunting Townhill Yard and
duties round the pits as well as short-haul coal trains.
Completing the freight tank engines was a J.88 0-6-0T
No.289 - Reid's first design in 1904 which was used on
goods traffic on the Charlestown branch, and finally
No.40, a little 0-4-0 saddle tank built at Cowlairs in
1897 to a design by Neilson & Co. No.40 spent most of
its time shunting at the gas works south of Dunfermline
Lower station and on the very sharply-curved Netherton
branch nearby. It was withdrawn in 1960 and was the last
engine of the class to work in Fife. The shed shunter
was Drummond 0-6-0T Class J.82 No.1335, which remained in
N.B. livery until it disappeared early in 1925.
    Included in the Dunfermline J.36 0-6-0s were two of
the 25 named engines of this class which had seen war
service in France from 1917 until 1919. No.662 'Bird-
wood' bore the name of a leading general while 'Ole Bill'
was a popular 'personality' representing the solid
British 'Tommy' in a series of cartoons by Bruce
Bairnsfather.
    Passenger services operated by Dunfermline Upper were
not spectacular but very essential at a time when road
transport of any description was limited and by no means
fast. It is difficult to realise that the contemporary
motorbus had solid tyres and that tarmacadam roads were
not universal, water-bound road surfaces being very
frequent. There was a good train service from both Dunfermline Upper and Lower stations to Thornton via
Halbeath, Crossgates and Cowdenbeath as well as frequent
round trips to Inverkeithing interconnecting with the
main line to the coast. Employed on these were rebuilt
Holmes 4-4-0s of Class D.31 (No.262, Nos.640-1 and

No.769) as well as Wheatley 2-4-0s of Class E.9 (No.1239
and No.1247). The branch line to Alloa via Kincardine
was worked from the Dunfermline end by 0-4-4Ts No.589 and
No.92 (Class G.9), while N.15 4-4-2Ts No.15 and No.26
were general passenger spares. The short branch to
Charlestown on the shores of the Forth was operated by
D.51 4-4-0T No.1426.

A double-ended shed with four roads providing cover
for about 25 locomotives, this was an ideal place for
morning photography, and a typical example of the larger
North British shed devoted mainly to freight traffic.

In the 'Locomotive News' dated 22 December 1922 there
were reports from several sources about a trial trip
between Waverley and Newcastle (Central). The train,
made up of thirteen E.C.J.S. corridors and the North
Eastern dynamometer car (a load of approximately 400
tons), was hauled by N.B. Atlantic No.510 'The Lord
Provost' with its own crew in charge throughout. Said to
be the outcome of differing opinions about the performance of N.E. Atlantics on the Cockburnspath bank with its
stretches of 1 in 96, the result of the test was not made
public and a really proper comparison was impossible, as
the engine did not have water pick-up apparatus at the
time, so a stop had to be made at Berwick to replenish.
Whatever the real reason behind this interesting event it
is obvious that the authorities of both railways had the
impending future well in mind, and thoughts about greater
engine power on this tricky route.

By August 1923 locomotive tests between Newcastle and
Edinburgh took a definite step forward when the contend-
ers were Ivatt Atlantic No.1447N, Raven three-cylinder
Atlantic No.733 and North British Atlantic No.9878
'Hazeldean', fitted with water pick-up apparatus.
No.1447N was a very different-looking engine from the
Ivatt Atlantic familiar to the railway enthusiast for so
many years with its cab and boiler mountings reduced some
6" to comply with the N.B. loading gauge of 13', the most
restricted on the L.N.E.R. To begin with the engine
looked much bigger and more powerful. The tests were
made on the down 'Flying Scotsman' and I well remember
how splendid No.1447N looked, with the shorter funnel and
a proper curved roof on the cab replacing the typical
Doncaster style which to us resembled bent-over sheet
metal. Particularly striking and very 'English' was the
circular smokebox extended well ahead of the supporting

saddle, and so different from the narrow-waisted style
which predominated in Scotland apart from the recently-
built Highland 'Clans'.

The North Eastern Atlantic like 1447N was painted in
the new livery, while 'Hazeldean' had recently been
painted in its old bronze green with the new lettering
and number on its tender. Again no results were immediately published, but in due course it became known that
the N.B. entrant had put up the best performance. The
heavy coal consumption normally associated with the N.B.
Atlantic appears to have been reasonable, due undoubtedly
to 'Hazeldean' being in charge of its own driver, Tom
Henderson, destined to be the first Haymarket driver to
man a Gresley Pacific regularly in Newcastle. Although
1447N came third - understandably so with its small
cylinders - it certainly held the stage that exciting
week.

Another interesting visitor to Edinburgh in early 1923
was No.2400, the first of the Raven Pacifics which
appeared from time to time on test runs, painted in shop
grey and fully lined out in black and white. As far as
appearance went, and this is what mattered most to the
younger enthusiast in those days, I rather liked it. In
general terms No.2400 was an elongated Raven Atlantic,
but outstandingly striking was the vast boiler with a
barrel length of 26' and outside diameter of 6', the
latter resulting in a short and shapely chimney. The
standard six-wheeled tender was ridiculously out of proportion to a total engine and tender length of 72' 7"
over buffers, and the inside bearings to the trailing
wheels, similar to 'The Great Bear' (which I had had the
good fortune to see and photograph in 1921), also seemed
very out of date. Nevertheless it was Darlington's final
expression of the express locomotive and the largest I
had ever set eyes on. No thought was given to their
being anything else but first-class performers. Before
the year was out No.2400 was running in L.N.E.R. green
and the second of the class, No.2401, appeared from
Doncaster in North Eastern livery which it retained for
over twelve months.

Fort William had been chosen for our annual holiday in
August largely because it was somewhere completely new to
us all but because also some of the family wanted to
climb Ben Nevis. It was to be very different in many
ways from our customary holiday haunts on the Highland

Railway or at Ballater on Deeside, and it certainly
proved to be so from the railway point of view. Truth to
tell up to then I had never been farther west than the
platform ends at St. Enoch station, and my only view of
the famous River Clyde had been from the Jamaica Street
Bridge a few yards from Central station!

The West Highland was then a very new railway, construction having started simultaneously in 1889 at
Craigendoran, Arrochar, Crianlarich and Tyndrum. After
five long and arduous years' work in remote, rough and
rocky country the 100 miles of single line route to Fort
William was completed in 1894, with the formal opening
taking place in August of that year. It appears to have
been the first instance in this country of 100 miles of
railway coming into use in one day. Needless to say, on
that memorable occasion the engine was a 'West Highland
Bogie', one of Matthew Holmes' little 5' 7" 4-4-0s,
coupled to a train of coaches which had been specially
built for the service. Some of these, we discovered,
were still in use on the Mallaig extension. The design
incorporated single compartments at each end and a large
saloon in the centre with very ample windows, the aim
being to provide a maximum window area throughout and so
enabling a large proportion of the passengers to have a
window seat, a great asset in such splendid scenery.
Another desirable feature was the provision of toilet
facilities.

Fort William was a long expedition from Inverkeithing
and the journey started on an early morning train from
Thornton to Glasgow which was in charge of No.385, one
of Reid's second batch of 'Intermediate' 4-4-0s built in
1909. With 6' driving wheels they were the forerunners
of the famous 'Glens'.

Those acquainted with Queen Street station, which was
built as long ago as 1842, will know that it has been the
custom for many years for the West Highland trains to use
one of the two short platforms at the south side of the
station outside the spectacular main arch. The low overall roof and narrow platforms gave the impression of an
entirely separate station which tended to merge with the
adjoining goods station. Advertisements for hotels and
other West Highland attractions and a notice in 'the
Gaelic' directing incoming passengers from the Isles to
the enquiry office added to the atmosphere of this dark
corner of Queen Street.

Our train, the 11.25 a.m., was headed by No.496 'Glen Moidart', built in 1920 and the last of the 'Glen' Class. Composed of a mere five coaches, these were yet another more modern design specially built for the West Highland. It will be remembered that Reid in 1907 had introduced luxurious corridor sets as an answer to the Caledonian twelve-wheeled Grampian corridors. Seven years later a shortened edition 52' 7" in length, with the high elliptical roof and same general profile, were turned out for the Fort William trains. There were no vestibules, the side corridors leading into compartments at each end which had two windows in the gable ends, a custom which died hard on each of the three railways serving the Scottish Highlands. Although intended to increase the passengers' view - in practice, as in earlier examples - these served little purpose. An interesting point about the coach ends was that they included the normal outline of an opening for a flexible gangway with solid panels replacing the customary door, suggesting that Cowlairs were making use of their standard corridor coach end.

Various writers have described the West Highland Railway in the last thirty years or so, so comments on this journey 55 years ago will be comparatively brief. The utter strangeness of what lay ahead was perhaps an advantage.

After the 1½-mile climb to Cowlairs through the smoky Queen Street tunnel, we proceeded at a fairly brisk speed through the Glasgow suburbs, reaching the Clyde at Bowling and continuing along its shores to Craigendoran, where the river widens into a firth. Here was the base of the North British Clyde steamer fleet and we were able to distinguish the 'Lucy Ashton', 'Talisman', and the flagship 'Waverley' - later to be lost in the Dunkirk evacuation of 1940. The North British red funnel with its black top and white band is still to the fore on a post-Second World War 'Waverley' now operated by a preservation society and still giving great pleasure to the public.

At Craigendoran Junction we left the Helensburgh line and turning to the right met realities with an immediate gradient of 1 in 58. In a very short time it became evident why the run to Fort William was going to take well over four hours, as although there were occasional downhill stretches and even a short level at Shandon, there were long stretches of 1 in 54 on the stiff pull

to the 560' summit at Glen Douglas. Fascinating views of
'Glen Moidart' hard at work were no problem thanks to the
very sharp curves - the reason for the 40 m.p.h. speed
restriction throughout the entire route, which was even
less in certain places.

I have always thought the finest prospect from the
West Highland Railway is on the descent from Glen Douglas
to Arrochar and Tarbet where, running on a ledge 500'
above Loch Long in addition to beautiful views of the
loch itself, it is possible to look over to the entrance
to Glen Croe and see parts of the road leading to the
summit at 'Rest and be Thankful'. Directly opposite also
are the 'Arrochar Alps', the most prominent being Ben Ime
(3,318'), the highest Ben Vane, and Ben Arthur - better
known as 'The Cobbler'. In a guide book dated 1907 the
North British Railway goes to town with this excellent
story about this mountain:

> 'Near the summit of this massive Ben, the
> rocks show a formation, which seen from one
> side brings to the mind the picture of a
> giant cobbler at work at his craft. From
> another vantage-ground this "hill shoemaker"
> presents the appearance of resting from his
> labours. The resemblances are not too
> apparent, however, without a "local"
> companion ready to draw his attention to the
> phenomenon at the exact moment of time,
> although certainly, the conformation of the
> rocks is marvellous enough to attract the
> eye without the conjunction of the "pretty
> cobbler" story.'

Unfortunately, I have never had the company of a 'local
companion', but nevertheless it is a very striking mountain, which when the sun is setting in the west can
sometimes be seen from as far away as the Forth Bridge.

Other interesting tit-bits from this old railway guide
are that a ham-and-egg breakfast on a Clyde steamer cost
less than ten present-day pence, and a quarter-gill of
whiskey only three of the pennies of long ago.

Arrochar & Tarbet station serves the villages of
Arrochar at the head of Loch Long, and to the east across
a narrow isthmus of land Tarbet on the shores of Loch
Lomond, which the railway then followed for a distance of
eight miles to Ardlui, the station at the north end of

the loch. From here started the stiff pull up Glen
Falloch, eight miles of gradients almost continuously at
1 in 60 or so, to Crianlarich which we reached at about
1.30 p.m. There were of course no restaurant cars in
those days and sufficient standing time was allowed for a
quick lunch, on this occasion prolonged for twenty
minutes. The refreshment room, noted for its excellence,
also supplied refreshment baskets which one could order
in advance by advising the guard at Craigendoran.

Situated on the main road from the south to Oban and
Fort William, Crianlarich was an important local centre
as well as being the junction for the Callendar & Oban
line with which there was a connecting spur for interchange of goods traffic. It also boasted a small engine
shed where we observed No.663, a rebuilt Holmes 0-6-0
with a very substantial tender cab. This engine remained
closely associated with the West Highland until at least
twenty years ago, possibly longer. Waiting to cross us
on the up line was No.407 'Glen Beasdale', a 'Glen' we
had never seen on the east side of the country.

About six miles farther north between Tyndrum and
Bridge of Orchy and eagerly anticipated lay the famous
Horse Shoe Curve, its position easily identified well in
advance unless the clouds were low by the graceful cone
of Ben Doran, 3,523' high. In order to avoid the heavy
costs of crossing a broad valley the line was routed due
east then north across its head on two short viaducts,
then west along the lower slopes of Ben Doran itself
before resuming its northerly course. This deviation
added 1½ miles to the journey, all part of the policy to
keep as low as possible the cost of a railway through a
sparsely populated part of the country. Looking from
the carriage window it was extraordinary to see what
appeared to be another 'railway' directly opposite, and
my first thought was that we had rejoined the Callendar
& Oban line, last seen far below us at Tyndrum and now
far to the southwest.

On the twenty miles crossing of wild Rannoch Moor,
mostly 1,000' or so above sea level and ten miles from
remote Rannoch station, lies the highest point on the
line - Courrour (1,347') - and for the next twenty miles
to Spean Bridge, the junction for Fort Augustus, the
running is continuously downhill along the entire length
of Loch Treig and beyond, with intermediate stations at
Tulloch and Roy Bridge. Running along the hills high

above Roy Bridge we could see trains on the 3' gauge line
built in connection with the adits for the tunnel (fifteen miles long and 15' in diameter) destined to carry
water from Loch Treig right under Ben Nevis to a vast
hydro-electric power station at Fort William. This
remote little railway had a total length of twenty miles
and was operated mainly by Hunslet 4-6-0 tanks bearing
appropriate names, including 'Prince Charlie' and 'Flora
MacDonald'.

On the final ten miles from Spean Bridge we had
magnificent views of the tremendous precipices on the
north face of Ben Nevis, and journey's end, Fort William,
was finally reached just after four o'clock.

The West Highland station, all island platform style
with three exceptions, was very attractive. With very
deep eaves, the single-storey buildings were faced with
wooden shingles which had been specially imported from
Switzerland, apparently with the idea of presenting a
chalet style to harmonise with the surrounding mountains.
The result was very pleasing indeed. Between Fort
William's main street and Loch Linnhe there was just room
for a small station with two short platforms, one double-
faced, with an extension leading to MacBraynes Pier. The
junction for Mallaig (known as Mallaig Junction) a mile
or so down the line lay facing Fort William, so all
through traffic to Mallaig had to reverse - which in the
case of passenger trains imposed a considerable strain on
the station's limited resources. A short distance from
the junction was the engine shed.

It did not take long to discover that Fort William was
not an exhilarating railway centre. I have forgotten the
exact timing of the trains, but those prevailing in 1923
had continued as a general pattern over a long period.

In the up direction the first arrival of the day was
about 8.45 a.m., an all stations from Mallaig, followed
an hour later by another slightly faster having omitted
stops at Locheilside, Corpach and Banavie, the three
stations nearest to Fort William. This provided a quick
connection with the first train to the south, the 9.36
a.m. A third train from Mallaig arrived about 2.30 p.m.
with through coaches for Glasgow, these being attached tc
the last train for the south leaving about 3 p.m. This
also had sleeping cars and coaches for Kings Cross, due
to arrive there at seven o'clock next morning. I frequently saw them side-tracked in the Waverley for the

best part of an hour waiting to continue their journey on
a night sleeper to Kings Cross. The concluding train in
the up direction was a final all-stations from Mallaig
arriving about 7.30 p.m. At 10.15 a.m. the first down
train arrived with through portions which had left Kings
Cross at seven o'clock the previous evening. A portion
of this train continued to Mallaig. Due about 3.50 p.m.
was the train on which we had travelled from Glasgow. An
hour later another local to Mallaig, and finally at 8.15
the last train from the south - the 3.46 p.m. from Glasgow to Mallaig, the timing of which remained unaltered
for many years. There was always a considerable audience
waiting for the 3.46, whether to meet friends, get the
Glasgow evening newspaper, or merely to look. As it left
for the west behind Mallaig's own 'Glen' (at that time
No.256 'Glen Douglas'), one sensed the indefinable atmosphere associated with the last train of the day always
apparent in areas far distant from the busy centres, and
my brother and I were not alone when we waited to see the
train running along the far side of Loch Linnhe and
disappearing into the hills beyond Corpach. Darkness
would have fallen when 'Glen Douglas' reached its little
shed on the Sound of Sleet after its hour-and-a-half
journey.

We had two weeks at Fort William and, inevitably, with
such a sparse train service and the indifferent sort of
weather all too often experienced close to Ben Nevis, my
photography was restricted. There was, however, one
successful morning at the shed when present were: No.256
'Glen Roy', No.406 'Glen Croe', No.242 'Glen Mamie' in
L.N.E.R. green, No.495 'Glen Mallie', and No.256 'Glen
Douglas'. A special bonus for the West Highland was
Holmes' 'seven-footer' 4-4-0 No.603, which had been
called in to assist a heavy train from the south. Her
measured stride must have made a pretty picture as she
followed along behind the smaller-wheeled 'Glen'.
Finally, at the shed were two rebuilt Holmes 0-6-0s,
which one could never get away from, and a real treasure,
No.1390, one of the three 4-4-0Ts with 6' driving wheels
built by Dugald Drummond in 1879. Unfortunately, this
latter was out of steam and in a hopeless position for
photography. I had never seen one of these engines
before - nor since, for that matter - and to my lasting
regret did not have the courage to ask anyone if they
would shift it for a photograph.

Our visit to Mallaig was on a day excursion made up of
somewhat elderly bogie coaches with extremely narrow
corridors designed by Holmes, in charge of No.492 'Glen
Gau', assisted by a Holmes rebuilt 0-6-0. The former's
name was apparently a case of misspelling as, after
thorough searching by keen map readers, no glen of this
name could be found. In 1925 No.492 became 'Glen Gour'.
All in all, this was a magnificent trip on what is, without qualification, Britain's most scenic railway.

The construction of the line west from Fort William
known as the Mallaig Extension commenced in 1897, was
opened for traffic on 1 April 1901, with a ruling
gradient of 1 in 40 and the same maximum permissible
speed of 40 m.p.h. Travelling through rough country with
even more numerous steep ups and downs, it was a far
tougher proposition than the West Highland. There were
many cuttings through hard rock and as many as eleven
tunnels, the longest being one of 350 yards at Borrodale.
Most striking perhaps is Glenfinnan Viaduct, situated in
magnificent scenery deep in the mountains. One of the
earliest examples of reinforced concrete construction on
a big scale, it is just over 400 yards in length and 100'
high with 21 50' arches. Built on a sharp curve entailing a speed restriction of 25 m.p.h., there is plenty of
time to view and photograph Loch Shiel, with the monument
to Bonnie Prince Charles' '45 Jacobite uprising in the
foreground. Another gem is the first view of the
Cuillins of Rhum and Skye on the final run into Mallaig.

A visit to Fort Augustus, a matter of 24 miles from
Spean Bridge, was not unduly interesting. Initially a
locally promoted company known as the Invergarry & Fort
Augustus Railway, this was opened on 2 February 1903,
having taken five years to construct. Always in financial difficulties, it had no engines or rolling stock of
its own, and for a time under a financial arrangement
between the two companies the Highland Railway provided
these. Reaching their sphere of operation involved a
long journey from Perth through the centre of Scotland
to Spean Bridge. At different times the Highland engines
were No.48, a 'Skye Bogie', and one of David Jones'
4-4-0Ts, No.52, built in 1893. In 1907 this arrangement
ceased when the North British took over, finally purchas-
ing the company in 1914 - after experiencing many
problems, including complete closure of the line from
1911 to 1914. On our visit the branch engine was 0-4-4T

No.390, coupled to a mixed train which included a gas
tank wagon and one passenger coach. The only other
evidence of public transport was MacBrayne's paddle
steamer 'Gondolier' which in the summer made a daily
return trip through the Caledonian Canal from Inverness
to Banavie, a mile-and-a-half from Fort William. The
Fort Augustus branch was closed to all traffic except for
one weekly coal train on 1 December 1933, and completely
on 31 December 1946.

My final railway expedition from Fort William started
off by sea by a day excursion to Oban on David Mac-
Brayne's 'Fusilier'. Also a paddle steamer, she was a
dainty little thing of 776 tons with clipper bow and
bowsprit, built in 1888 of iron and steel. The sail to
Oban was excellent but the Caledonian shed there was
practically deserted, producing a McIntosh 4-6-0 'Oban
Bogie', an 0-4-4T used on the Ballachulish branch, and
fortunately one of Pickersgill's new 4-6-0s for the Oban
line, which made a pleasing photograph. This was my
first visit to Oban.

Our West Highland holiday added only twelve photographs to my railway collection, but the experience of
travelling on the line for the first time was never to be
forgotten; and incidentally we did reach the summit of
Ben Nevis, continually enveloped in low cloud entered
some 700' up from the traditional starting point at
Achintee Farm.

The rapid development of the British Aluminium
Company's hydro-electric complex in Lochaber and the
final completion of the aluminium manufacturing works at
Fort William had a dramatic effect on rail traffic, both
passenger and freight increasing greatly, and the year
1929 saw the advent of restaurant cars on the line. Ex-
East Coast twelve-wheeled clerestories running with
standard N.B. main line vestibuled stock rather belied
the necessity for the shorter coaches hitherto used.
Another innovation was Sunday excursions, initially from
Queen Street. According to the press these were ill-
received by the local inhabitants of Fort William, who
showed their displeasure by closing their shops and
pulling down the house blinds. This attitude changed in
time and in high season there could be as many as five of
these trains heading for the northwest from Glasgow,
Edinburgh, Fife and other centres in the south. The day
fare from Queen Street to Fort William was seven shil-

lings and, for a further two shillings, Mallaig. Forty
miles on a return fare of twenty decimal pence. . . .
    Helping the 'Glens' were a number of Gresley K.2
2-6-0s which with 5' 9" driving wheels were ideal for the
job. Later they were to be fitted with side window cabs
and to be named after well-known lochs.
    The railway scene at Fort William has changed consid-
erably in recent years. To relieve congestion in the
main street, the only route from south to north, a new
station has been built three-quarters of a mile to the
north replacing the former terminus which, with its
approach lines, has been demolished, thus providing space
for dual road carriageways avoiding the busy centre of
the town. In common with modern ideas the station is
adjacent to the bus station.
    In September it became known that the London Midland
& Scottish Railway had chosen Derby red as their engine
and carriage livery - which I remember came as a great
surprise to many of us, chiefly I think because we were
still thinking in terms of Crewe and the West Coast
Route. Once again the colours of one of the former
companies had been chosen; after all, the L.N.E.R. with
very minor alterations had followed Great Northern practice, although the varnished teak coach had been familiar
for many years as far north as Aberdeen and Inverness and
its impact was going to be far less than L.M.S. red.
    Another announcement was entirely new numbering for
L.M.S. engine stock. In blocks of thousands the former
Midland locomotives were allocated 1 to 4999, with 14000
to 17000 for the former Scottish companies. To think of
Caledonian No.903 'Cardean' as No.14752 was to us quite
shattering and it was perhaps fortunate that the name had
been dispensed with by that time. In general terms in
Scotland, passenger engines had numbers in the 14000
range, passenger tank engines had numbers in the 15000
range, whilst mixed traffic, goods, tender and tank were
numbered from 16000 to 17000. It was an exciting thought
to contemplate these vast numbers but it soon became a
habit to refer to an engine quite simply as, for example,
fourteen two eight two - a 'Skye Bogie'.
    On a final summer visit to Perth the only signs of
change were new notice boards, etc., as hitherto, and the
absence of the Highland crest on freshly green painted
'Clans' and 'Castles' still, however, with H.R. on their
tenders. I also noticed that the short-lived North

British dining car to Blair Atholl on the afternoon train
from Perth had been replaced by one from the L.M.S. St.
Rollox appeared to have ceased complete repainting,
patching up being the order of the day.

About the same time a new L.N.E.R. engine classification system was inaugurated in which a letter represented
the wheel arrangement and the number which followed the
actual class, regardless of origin. Based on Great
Northern practice, their former engines headed the list,
e.g., an Ivatt Atlantic was C.1; and such was the
variety of Atlantics on the L.N.E.R. that C.11 was
reached before Reid's masterpiece received its new identification. Needless to say, the letter A applied to
Pacifics.

The North British already had its own classification
based on power output, at times somewhat ambiguous -
especially in the case of the letter M, which was shared
by Classes D.31 4-4-0, C.15 and C.16 4-4-2Ts, and Reid's
G.8 0-4-4T. All were capable of the same work but had
very different coal and water capacities. The small
plate bearing the N.B. letter appeared above the number
plates, some of which were still in evidence even after
Nationalisation.

Before returning to school I had the usual autumn week
at Aberdeen, including two very successful mornings at
Kittybrewster shed. Most of the engines present carried
the letters L. & N.E.R. and large numerals but still
retained the Great North red-and-yellow lining.
Completely revarnished, they had all the appearance of
complete repaints - very much smarter than No.108s, which
had been turned out in the L.N.E.R. black with a single
red line.

Idling about the shed with ash wagons was our old
friend, brass-domed 4-4-0 No.45A, now with its two
companions of 1866, No.44A, classified D.47/2, and
(awaiting its final visit to Inverurie) Class D.47/1
No.49A, built ten years later. Unfortunately No.49A was
withdrawn only a few months after I had photographed her.

Most interesting on this visit to Kittybrewster was
D.43 Manson 4-4-0 No.9, still with smokebox wingplates and
built up Stirling-type funnel, which I had not seen since
Ballater days in 1914 and had long considered extinct. A
mixture of ideas was a smaller Manson, No.6 (Class D.46),
with smokebox wingplates and the standard shapely chimney
introduced by Johnson when he joined the Great North from

Derby in 1890. No.5 and No.6, the only two of their
class, were the first new engines built at Kittybrewster
and originally bore the names 'Kinmundy' and 'Thomas
Adam', these respectively being the name of the residence
of the then chairman and of the vice chairman himself.

The new school term brought with it the advantages of
a season ticket to Edinburgh, which I had not seen for
two long months. There were quite a few changes, notable
being how the Edinburgh suburban sets had been greatly
improved by the new North Eastern coaches first introduced earlier in the year. There were also more green
engines about, two outstanding beauties being No.869B
'Bonnie Dundee' and No.902B 'Highland Chief'. Less
attractive were Reid's 'Intermediate' 4-4-0s (now D.32
and D.33) which looked very drab in black with the single
and rather thin red line. On the other hand, black tank
engines presented a neat appearance with the lettering
and large number adding a welcome splash of colour to the
tank sides. There was still nothing to report from
Princes Street station.

November saw the first visit of a Gresley Pacific to
Edinburgh, this being No.1481N, which was then engaged in
trials based on Gateshead shed. She was the last of a
batch of ten put into service in 1923 commencing with
No.1472, subsequently named 'Flying Scotsman', to repre-
sent the L.N.E.R. at the British Empire Exhibition at
Wembley in 1924. Considerable alterations had to be made
to the engine to accommodate North British loading gauge
restrictions - only 12' 11" compared with 13' 6" on the
Great Northern. As a matter of interest, there was
special dispensation between Berwick and Edinburgh for
North Eastern engines with funnel heights of 13' 3".
Consequently No.1481N had her boiler mountings severely
cut down in addition to considerable alterations to the
cab. At first sight she struck me as huge, at the same
time very ugly, due entirely to the funnel which had been
lowered simply by machining off 2" from the top rim,
resulting in a shapeless mess. However, forgetting this
- which after all was a temporary expedient - she was a
splendid-looking engine, and the first visit of a Gresley
Pacific to Scotland was a historic event and for us an
excellent finale to the first year of the Grouping. It
is difficult now to realise that 55 years ago Pacifics
were very rare indeed.

VII
THE GROUPING - 1924

Towards the end of January, there occurred a very interesting example of the L.N.E.R.'s obvious determination to increase their passenger traffic receipts. For two years past the Caledonian had been successfully wooing Glasgow Rugby Union supporters attending the internationals at Murrayfield by running special day return trains composed entirely of Pullman cars. On 25 February 1922, for instance, the train leaving Glasgow (Central) at 11 a.m. and returning in the early evening after the match consisted of an L.N.W.R. passenger brake and seven Pullmans. Including the observation car from the Oban line, 'Maid of Morven', this comprised seven of the ten Pullmans then operated by the company.

Although the North British had done its best to compete with some of its total fleet of nine dining cars, their best efforts bore no comparison with their rival's enterprise and it was a bitter pill for their supporters to swallow. On the first international of the season in January 1924 we were delighted to see that the two restaurant cars on the 6 p.m. to Queen Street had been increased to four, while waiting in the down main at Waverley for Dundee and Aberdeen was a magnificent cavalcade of eleven restaurant cars from each of the former railways, North British, North Eastern, Great Northern and even one Great Central. This train ran ahead of the normal 6.35 p.m. to Aberdeen, which also had extra refreshment facilities.

I usually paused at Haymarket station for an hour or so on my way home to see these specials go by, especially the super train for Aberdeen. It was a thrilling sight to see it passing through the dimly lit station, Atlantic- and 'Scott'-hauled, windows all steamed up, and emitting a delightful odour of bacon and eggs. There must have been many high teas and other refreshments enjoyed that evening; a happy journey for both passengers and attendants, particularly if the right team had won. This certainly showed what the considerable resources of the L.N.E.R. could do, and our thoughts turned yet again to what lay ahead in the locomotive field. Something had to be done soon, as of the 1,074

engines passed by the N.B. to the new company, 200 were
on the duplicate list and aging rapidly.

In February I had my first brief view of a Caledonian
engine in the new red livery running light on the over-
bridge on the Leith and Barnton lines near Haymarket,
referred to earlier in these pages. At the north end of
this bridge was Murrayfield signal box which controlled
points completing a triangle which was frequently used
for turning engines working into Princes Street station.
This ceased with the lifting of various lines when
Princes Street was closed and West Coast traffic
diverted to Waverley via Haymarket. On the following day
the red engine was traced to Princes Street station and
found to be Dunalistair II 4-4-0 No.14238. The red was
quite nice but the finish was not up to previous St.
Rollox standards, and the unlined boiler looked very
plain indeed. The large numbers on the tender however
were very attractive, and also the new L.M.S. crest on
the cab side. Incorporating a portion of the arms of
London - a dragon surmounted by a St. George's Cross -
along with the rose of England and the thistle of Scotland, all encircled by the name of the company in full,
this was a masterpiece of simplicity and expression.
Also standing at the station was a small wheeled 0-4-4
Balerno tank (No.15151) in red livery, and completing an
L.M.S. trio a Drummond 0-6-0 goods engine in the new
black livery. In unlined black with large numerals on
the tender, it had on the cab side the letters L.M.S. in
yellow on a red panel, somewhat reminiscent of the old
L.N.W.R. number plate.

Ere long we were to see red engines quite frequently,
as well as coaches in the new colour. These were probably an improvement on the old lake-and-white which,
despite all the glamorous opinions expressed by various
writers in the past, did not wear at all well.

February also ushered in the first L.N.E.R. numbering
scheme. In this, former North Eastern engines retained
their present numbers, the other constituent companies
adding blocks of thousands, these being: Great Northern
- 3000, Great Central - 5000, Great Eastern - 7000, and
the North British - 9000. The Great North came along at
the end of the G.C. by adding 6800 - for example, No.47
'Sir David Stewart' became No.6847 while on the N.B.,
No.898 'Sir Walter Scott' became No.9898, and 'Old
Wheatley' No.1249 retired as No.10249. This arrangement

had its faults and led to a completely new scheme in 1943 in which numbers were directly related to the engine classes.

Other signs of change on the L.N.E.R. were the new station colours of brown and cream and also the adoption of the North Eastern pattern of poster board in black, headed by a bright red panel with raised white-painted letters. Station names on cast-iron plates, again with raised letters, were inserted on station seats instead of the former painted names.

Generally photography started early in April, any attempts earlier in the year in weaker sunlight producing with the standard of film then available an effect known as 'scot and whitewash'. It is extraordinary to think that in the 'last days of steam' enthusiasts were actually looking for such effects; with very striking results!

Consequently the first shed visit of the year was late in March to Haymarket, which had quite a good layout for photography but was cramped at the east end, where the spurs leading into the shed roads were very short. A favourite stance for engines, a loop next to the up Fife main line, was dangerous, and the shed staff made it clear that it was out of bounds - otherwise, it was 'oot ye go'. The turntable would not take anything larger than a 4-4-0 so that N.B. or N.E. Atlantics had to use the Gorgie triangle.

Haymarket was an important shed providing motive power mainly for passenger services, these in degree of import-ance being: the main line to Aberdeen; engine-changing at Dundee; Glasgow (Queen Street) via Falkirk, and the secondary line through Bathgate; over the Forth Bridge via Alloa to Stirling; semi-fast and stopping trains to Dundee direct, or round the East of Fife line via Anstruther and St. Andrews. The following list gives some idea of the locomotive strength around 1924 (N.B. numbers have been used, as at that time few had received the additional 9000).

Leading the way were five Atlantics: No.874 'Dunedin', No.875 'Midlothian', No.877 'Liddesdale', No.878 'Hazeldean', and No.510 'The Lord Provost'. The Atlantics were of course reserved for the Aberdeen road. Next in line for the express service to Glasgow (Queen Street) were six D.30 superheated 'Scotts': No.411 'Dominie Sampson', No.412 'Laird o'Monkbarns', No.414

'Dugald Dalgetty', No.415 'Claverhouse', No.416
'Ellangowan', and No.428 'Adam Woodcock'. Three of the
original saturated 'Scotts' (Class D.29), No.338 'Helen
Macgregor', No.339 'Ivanhoe', and No.361 'Vich Ian Vhor',
were employed mainly on Dundee semi-fast and local
trains. The remaining engines were in a smaller cate-
gory, rebuilt Holmes 4-4-0s Class D.31 No.579, Nos.729-
30, and Nos.733-6, most of which had been at Haymarket
for many years. These were used on Stirling and Larbert
trains together with three rebuilt versions of Drummond's
4-4-0s built in the 1870s: D.27 No.1323, with the
Stirling round open cab, and D.28 No.1361 and No.1387,
with the standard side windows. Finally there were three
'seven-footers': No.595, No.596 and No.597, which were
used as pilots for the Atlantics on the Aberdeen trains
when the load exceeded 370 tons. Three C.15 4-4-2 tanks,
No.1, No.25 and No.141, were regular performers on the
short branch line from Ratho, joining the Glasgow and
Aberdeen lines via the little village of Kirkliston.
These tanks always took care of the Sunday morning and
evening trains from Waverley to Dunfermline Lower. Three
J.83 0-6-0 tanks including No.826 and No.828, employed as
west end shunters at Waverley, and one goods engine, a
J.35 (No.848), completed the Haymarket stud as I remember
it. There were no 'Glens' at Haymarket, and it must have
been one of the few sheds that did not have one of the
ubiquitous N.15 0-6-2 tanks at that time.
    Although thoroughly admired at the time, one had to
admit that it was not a very spectacular collection of
locomotives. Relying on an Atlantic originating in 1906
and the superheated 'Scott' of 1912, it compared very
indifferently with the post-war Caledonian and Highland
designs and G. & S.W.R. 'Baltics', ineffectual though
some of them were, and I have often wondered if N.B. (and
Great North) locomotive policy lagged after the war
simply because William Whitelaw knew considerably more
about impending events than his opposite numbers in Scotland.
    A three-hour stay at Haymarket on this first visit of
the year resulted in only nine photographs because of
lack of sunshine, but I had a nice picture of No.510
'The Lord Provost', which with No.9878 'Hazeldean' -
bronze green with the new number - had been fitted with
water pick-up apparatus and was taking regular night
turns to Newcastle along with the three Haymarket

'lodgers' - Raven three-cylindered Atlantics No.714, No.2193 and No.2194.

The first English engines to be transferred to the Southern Scottish area were not very thrilling, but it was a beginning. In May ten ex-North Eastern little 0-6-0s of Class J.24 came over the border. Of these four (No.1841, No.1952, No.1898 and No.1949) were allocated to Dunfermline Upper, where they replaced old Drummond 0-6-0s on the lightly laid branch lines serving the West Fife collieries. Their 4' 7" wheels were very suitable for this work and their drivers took quite kindly to them, being noticeably impressed by the comforts of their spacious cabs!

A visit to Perth in June revealed a complete transformation on the L.M.S., many of the engines seen on a visit to the south shed being in the new red livery - not least being superheated 4-4-0s of the Dunalistair IV and Pickersgill Classes. An interesting arrival was No.14762 'Clan Campbell', the first Highland engine I had seen in its new coat. Like Perth General station, the shed was a busy place during the rush hours but at other times unnaturally quiet, with hardly an engine moving. With a large layout it was a splendid place for photography. From three o'clock in the afternoon when the sun was getting into the right position there were only two hours still available to me, as a cycle run of 32 miles still lay ahead and I was expected home by nine. Nevertheless a lot could be done in that time if there were no clouds about, and I have many happy memories of watching the line of engines slowly moving towards the turntable, which provided an excellent stage.

Although an important centre Perth in railway terms was out on a limb, well away from the centre of things - and the variety of engine classes was very restricted, being geared chiefly to express passenger and freight traffic. Stationed there was No.959, the last of Pickersgill's three-cylindered 4-6-0s, and one of his 60 Class, No.65. These were joined by No.956 and No.64 working from Balornock. There was one 'Cardean', No.905, which seemed to be confined to the northern section to Aberdeen, and also No.49, one of McIntosh's two large 4-6-0s which preceded the 'Cardeans' in 1903. Completing the express passenger allocation were about twenty 4-4-0s of the superheated Dunalistair IV and Pickersgill Classes. Smaller Dunalistairs occasionally

came in as pilots. Two of the 'Sir James King' 4-6-0s,
with 5' 9" driving wheels (one being No.14618, fitted
experimentally in 1910 with a side-windowed cab), two of
their successors, McIntosh's last design of 1914, and an
ex-Highland 'River' were all used on fast freight. Local
goods trains were handled by McIntosh and Pickersgill
0-6-0s as well as by the smaller Drummond 0-6-0s later
known as 'Jumbos'.

A fleet of McIntosh 0-4-4 tanks, two of the small
Drummond 0-4-4 tanks with solid bogie wheels for the
Methven branch, some standard McIntosh 0-6-0 shunting
tanks and a 0-4-0 saddle tank for the harbour branch
completed Perth South shed's stud.

Among the last steam engines to use Perth South were
Pacifics transferred from Eastern and Scottish Region in
the early 1960s for use on the tightly-timed three-hour
expresses from Glasgow to Aberdeen - their final blaze of
glory on express passenger work. There are no signs of
the shed now, the site being occupied by a large Tesco
supermarket.

The Highland shed at Perth at which I also spent some
time also required an afternoon sun. It could be a busy
spot between two o'clock and three o'clock in the afternoon.

Waiting to take out the 3.50 p.m. for Inverness was
No.57 'Clan Cameron', with No.1 'Ben-y-Gloe' following on
the slow to Blair Atholl. Just arrived from Inverness
were No.51 'Clan Fraser' and No.14764 'Clan Munro'.
Standing in the yard were three 'Castles', No.50 'Brodie
Castle', No.143 'Gordon Castle' and No.149 'Duncraig
Castle'. Looking very lost without its tender was No.17
'Ben Alligan'. Inside the shed and thus out of range
were two Jones goods 4-6-0s and No.127 'Loch Garry'.

Perth shared equally with Inverness the eight 'Clans'
and eight Cumming goods 4-6-0s as well as having a few
'Castles' and Jones goods for the main line, with 'Lochs'
and 'Small Bens' for the 'Blair Slows'. There were also
three tank engines, a large Drummond 0-6-4T for local
goods, the station shunter 4-4-0 tank No.50B (No.15012)
and, most interesting of all, one of the three 0-6-0
outside-cylindered tanks built by Drummond in 1903.
Using 5' 3" driving wheels plus connecting rods and
motion from an old 2-4-0 goods type, and surplus boilers
built for another elderly 2-4-0 passenger class, they
were described by the railway press at the time as a

'pleasing mixture of the designs of Mr. Jones, the past, and Mr. P. Drummond, the present, locomotive superintendent'. The last of the three survived until 1932.

Somehow or other the shed staff and drivers at Perth North were not very forthcoming, unlike their opposite numbers in the Highlands whose kindness was hospitality itself; quite often one had to photograph engines as they were moving from the turntable to the shed. However there was little point in staying there very long, as it would be well into the evening before there were further signs of movement.

The former North British shed was seldom visited, mainly due to lack of time; also, there was nothing for the camera which was not obtainable nearer home. Naturally, its most important passenger duty was providing motive power for the main line to Edinburgh, and as I remember the scene in 1924 superheated 'Scott' No.418 'Dumbiedykes' and 'Glen' No.270 'Glen Garry' were employed on these services, with saturated 'Scotts' No.243 'Meg Merrilies' and No.244 'Madge Wildfire' understudying as necessary. For the Glasgow trains branching off at Kinross Junction via the Devon Valley line and Alloa there were four rebuilt Holmes 4-4-0s of Class D.31 including No.9214 and No.9574, while for the North Fife line there was a solitary Holmes 0-4-4 tank No.589 (G.7). The station shunter was an old Drummond 0-6-0 tank, No.1356, which was withdrawn in 1925 and replaced by a Holmes J.82 0-6-0 tank similar to the Waverley shunters.

The former N.B. shed at Perth will always be remembered for its splendidly polished engines. One driver in particular spent a lot of time decorating his engine's smokebox front. Every edge available had a polished rim and in addition the name of his engine, 'Glen Garry', appeared on the plating just below the smokebox door, all done by very careful removal of the paint using a stencil as a guide.

Early in August we set off on our annual summer holiday, this time at Aviemore. It was our first visit to the Highlands north of Perth since 1922, and we knew there would be many old friends missing. The L.M.S. had not taken long to decide about the most elderly members of the Highland family and had already withdrawn sixteen old 4-4-0s, five of the 'Strath' Class, and as many as eleven of the old 'Dukes'. With nothing to replace them from other sections the authorities at Inverness appeared to be carrying on quite happily.

The 11.50 a.m. from Perth with No.55 'Clan Mackinnon' at the head had a total load of ten bogies. Leading were two North British from Edinburgh, two Caledonian from Glasgow, an eight-wheeled Pullman, 'Lady Nairne', and finally four Highland coaches and a luggage brake - vestibuled throughout and a very smart turnout.

The maximum load for a 'Clan' on the fifteen-mile climb to Druimochdar Summit was 220 tons so, at Blair Atholl, 35 miles from Perth, we took on No.132 'Loch Naver' which, as we were not stopping at Dalnaspidal, saw us through to Dalwhinnie.

The entire journey of 82 miles from Perth to Aviemore is beautiful, but it is near Struan at the entrance to Glen Garry that heather moors take over from patchy little green fields, trees and hedges. Worth looking for at Calvine, four miles north of Blair, is the very interesting bridge where the railway simultaneously crosses the River Garry and the B487 road to Kinloch Rannoch, an arrangement forced on the engineers by the restricted location as well as problems with the local landowners. The original bridge - a graceful three-arched stone viaduct with castellated turrets on the pillars - harmonised splendidly with the nearby Falls of Garry. At the turn of the century the line was doubled and instead of widening the stone arches a separate lattice girder bridge was placed alongside them on the up river side. This certainly added to the interest of the bridge but was distinctly ugly in such a setting.

I suppose it is well over 35 years since the Falls of Garry disappeared and the river itself changed on its upper reaches from a roaring foaming torrent to a paltry little burn. If the passenger keeps a sharp lookout on the west side as the train gets nearer Dalnaspidal he will notice at intervals little aqueducts leading the waters of Garry into the hillside, and eventually to the hydro-electric power station at Pitlochry - probably best known as the place where the tourist can see, from an observation chamber, salmon on their journey from the sea to spawn! Fortunately time heals and the Garry, which the railway follows all the way to Dalnaspidal, is still very lovely in its moorland setting.

Aviemore, 692' above sea level, was always in the days of steam one of the most popular centres on the Highland Railway for the railway enthusiast, second only to

Inverness in interest. Its railway history dates back to
the 1860s, when on 3 August 1863 a section of the
projected line south over the Grampians reached there
from Forres. The resulting chain of events led to the
Highland main line between Perth and Inverness via Forres
and Nairn. It was not however until the end of the
century, with the opening of the direct line via Carr
Bridge in November 1898, that the station earned the
distinctive title of 'Aviemore Junction'.

In addition to being a busy junction - before the days
of the motor car - it had an important role as a locomotive depot. The Highland seldom went in for double-
heading their trains throughout - it is doubtful if they
had sufficient engines for this - and the custom was to
provide assistance over the main mountain passes. Aviemore had three of these to think about: southwards,
Druimochdar, 1,484'; northwards, Sloch Muich Pass on the
Carr Bridge line, 1,315'; and northwards again, Dava
Summit on the Forres line, 1,052'. These were in
distance from Aviemore approximately thirty, twelve and
eighteen miles respectively. Assisting engines were
always at the head of the train and were away from base
for lengthy periods, which required a fairly large number
of engines for these duties. As a matter of interest the
unassisted loads for a 'Clan' from Aviemore was 300 tons
for Druimochdar; Dava, 300 tons; and Slochd, 230 tons.
There was a nasty little bit of 1 in 60 on the Slochd!

In August 1924 the pilot engines, all 4-4-0s, were:
No.119 'Loch Insh', No.120 'Loch Ness', No.14383 'Loch-
an-Dorb', No.14388 'Loch Luichart', No.133 'Loch
Laoghal', No.7 'Ben Attow' and No.47 'Ben a'Bhuird'. Two
of the 'Lochs' were then in the new red livery.

Also stationed at Aviemore were No.140 'Taymouth
Castle', emergency engine for the main line, two Jones
goods 4-6-0s and a couple of 'Barneys', Drummond's 0-6-0s
of 1902.

Most interesting of all were three veterans standing
in sidings associated for many years with engines which
had finished their days. These were No.91A 'Strathspey',
built in 1892, and two old 'Dukes', No.79A 'Atholl' and
No.84A 'Dochfour', built respectively in 1886 and 1888.
The shed foreman who told us they had been there for a
year kindly arranged for 'Atholl' to be cleaned up for a
photograph but, unfortunately, all three were called
south before this could be done.

In common with the Highland Railway elsewhere Aviemore
had its busy moments when, for example, trains arrived
from Inverness via Carr Bridge and also from the old line
through Forres. Each had through coaches for Edinburgh
and Glasgow which had to be sorted out to simplify later
operations at Perth. Pullman cars which had terminated
their trips from the south at Aviemore had to be inserted
in the middle of the trains and watching the whole operation was most enjoyable. The last train for the south
left about 6 p.m. with through coaches and sleepers for
Euston and Kings Cross, a mere shadow of the 'Royal
Highlander' of later years.

A recent tour of the Highlands disclosed that Aviemore
station itself had altered very little apart from the
closure of one side of the island platform and the removal of a dock platform at the north end. The surrounding
layout, however, had been sadly reduced. Aviemore south
signal box has gone and the wooden pathway between the
rails which enabled the signalman to run across at the
last moment to 'catch the tablet' from a train arriving
from the south (regarded by many generations as a public
footpath) is now well and truly fenced off. The Strathspey Railway has revived the engine shed and, among other
plans, intends to install the former Kyle of Lochalsh
turntable in the existing rubble-filled pit.

Aviemore station is splendidly situated with Rothie-
murchus Forest and the High Tops of the Cairngorms in the
background, and in spite of all the changes it is still
nice on a summer evening to wander along to the station
to see the up 'Royal Highlander' depart for Euston behind
a Class 47 diesel.

It had been common knowledge for some time that the
L.N.E.R. had on order forty Gresley Pacifics, twenty from
Doncaster Works and a similar number from the North
British Locomotive Co. in Glasgow. It was also known
that five of these were destined for Haymarket. Consequently, having learned that the first five of the
Glasgow-built engines had actually arrived there, our
first shed visit after our return from the Highlands was
to Haymarket shed - on 23 August. The new engines were
numbered 2563-7, the first carrying the name 'William
Whitelaw'. The makeshift chimney carried by No.1481N had
been replaced by one still lower, in fact one 8½" in
height, and in my opinion the most shapely chimney
designed by Doncaster for many years. The cab roof was

slightly altered, as well as the ugly ventilator on
No.1481N, and the whole effect was magnificent - indeed,
more impressive than the original 'Great Northern' built
to the more generous Great Northern loading gauge. As
always the N.B. Locomotive Co. finish was superb. Apart
from the 'banjo' dome, which some railway students are
not very happy about, 'Flying Scotsman' (incredibly, the
only one of the class to be preserved) is a perfect
representative of the forty Gresley Pacifics delivered to
the company in 1924-25, a class which, with later
additions, was to become famous in the locomotive world.
They made a considerable impact on Haymarket and the men
were delighted with them. After initial running-in on
the Glasgow line they soon settled down to their intended
task, the East Coast main line to Newcastle, displacing
Haymarket's three North Eastern Raven Atlantics which,
however, still remained there as reserves. Two of the
Pacifics were given to North British men, one being the
well-known Tom Henderson who had blazed the North British
trail to Newcastle with Atlantic No.510 'The Lord
Provost' at the end of 1922. The other three went to the
North Eastern men at Haymarket. Introducing ex-N.B. men
to the Newcastle run was obviously most desirable. The
Pacifics also ran to Glasgow but were prohibited from
other ex-North British lines.

Yet another delight at the same time was the advent of
the Class D.11/2 4-4-0s, otherwise Great Central
'Improved Directors'. Twelve were ordered from Kitsons
of Leeds and a similar number from Armstrong Whitworth on
Tyneside. The 27 superheated 'Scotts' had been built
over a period of eight years and it was quite astonishing
that, in a matter of months, 24 of one of the premier
express 4-4-0 classes in the country were going to take
over the former engines' duties. With a Doncaster-style
chimney, not pure Ivatt fortunately, and very bare-
looking splashers with no brass edging or name, they
appeared very different from their handsome ancestors -
but with their high-pitched boilers, Belpaire fireboxes
and gracious styling, synonymous with the Great Central,
soon won our hearts; further, the low chimney gave them
the same 'big engine' look of the N.B. Atlantics. Their
numbers, 6378-6401 in the Great Central series, were
another novelty for us. Although their drivers were a
little chary of their 6' 9" driving wheels, 3" greater
than the 'Scotts' combined with the same 20" x 26"

cylinders - indeed both types bore the same N.B. classification letter J - the Scottish 'Directors' soon became
very popular. The first seven were immediately put to
work on the Edinburgh - Glasgow expresses, but it was not
until early in the following year that the order was
completed, when they were distributed to other sheds in
the area.

Another Great Central class came north at the same
time, and at Dunfermline Upper in August I got my first
photograph of one of the three ex-R.O.D. 2-8-0s attached
to this shed - No.6328, No.6290 and No.2691. In adapting
to the N.B. loading gauge Gorton Works had fitted one of
their lower Robinson chimneys, resulting in a very
purposeful-looking heavy freight engine. All three
retained the continental-style buffers, additional chain
link couplings on the buffer beams, and a couple of screw
jacks bolted on the running plate, all part of the equip-
ment required for use on the Continent. Classed 04,
these 2-8-0s were soon distinguishing themselves on the
Fife - Aberdeen coal trains, taking throughout the route
an average of seven more mineral wagons than a Class J.37
0-6-0. Their sphere of operation, which was very
limited, was subject to the following general conditions:
1) they must not be double-headed; 2) their speed must
not exceed 30 m.p.h.; and 3) they must not work into
colliery sidings. Another embargo, presumably due to
length of sidings, was that trains terminating at Dundee
should not exceed fifty wagons plus a brake van.

Our photographic year more or less closed with the
annual September visit to Kittybrewster, the last for a
few years, as long school holidays had ended and an
office life lay ahead. Little No.45A - photographed for
the last time - was still there with its loco-coal and
ash wagons.

The second year of the Grouping had been very
interesting, especially on my home ground, and fortunately the weather had been very kind to the camera.

VIII
THE GROUPING - 1925

Early in 1925 the L.N.E.R. published a small book entitled 'The Flying Scotsman - The World's Most Famous Train', which traced back to June 1862 the date at which the 'Scotch' express from Kings Cross became the 'Ten o'Clock' - prior to which time it had departed at times varying from 9 to 9.30 a.m. Apparently however there was no record available as to when and by whom it was named 'Flying Scotsman'. One possibility was that it might have developed from the fastest day train on the East Coast route being called the 'Flying Scotch Express'.

What was probably more interesting at the time was an indication of future publicity which appeared in the introduction. In this the writer stated that, although not in the public timetable, the title 'Flying Scotsman' had recently been given 'a degree of official sanction' with the naming of Gresley Pacific No.1472 (as she then was) in time for exhibition at the British Empre Exhibition at Wembley in 1924. This early L.N.E.R. publication, well informed and containing over fifty photographs, cost exactly one shilling! One very interesting chapter illustrated the locomotive types involved, ranging from single-driving wheeled engines through the 2-4-0 and 4-4-0 Classes to the Atlantic era. Three photographs to a page compared Great Northern, North Eastern and North British designs. Continuing on the same theme 'Pacific type locomotives' had 'Flying Scotsman', built to G.N. loading gauge as she appeared at Wembley, 'City of York', a tribute to Sir Vincent Raven, and rather ingeniously representing the North British Haymarket's new Pacific 'William Whitelaw' - which after all bore the name of a Scot and had been built in Scotland!

It was clear that the L.N.E.R. intended to name at least one of their premier express trains and very soon the 'Ten o'Clock' was distinguished with a 'Flying Scotsman' board on every coach and, helpful to passengers, a smaller board bearing their destinations - four in all: Edinburgh, Aberdeen, Glasgow and Perth, with Kings Cross on the reverse sides. A further development had been the building in 1924 of a completely new train which included a 'triplet' restaurant car, first and third, with kitchen

in the centre. Electricity took the place of gas for
cooking. This replaced the new train of 1914 in which
the kitchen car, the only vehicle in the train to use
gas, was a separate car of all-steel construction. The
new train consisted of nine ordinary coaches plus the
articulated restaurant car, and with a Gresley Pacific at
the head was a very impressive sight.

It was not long before all 24 'Directors' were
delivered and working from Haymarket, Eastfield, St. Margaret's and Dundee, with two at Perth. Those at
Haymarket, primarily intended for the Glasgow line, were
used when necessary as substitutes for Atlantics on the
Aberdeen road, but invariably on the heavier trains which
had a pilot in any case. The two Perth 'Directors'
(Nos.6387-8), always spotlessly clean, were special
favourites as they took me to Edinburgh every day and one
occasionally had a trip in the cab. Later in the spring,
much to our surprise and absolutely unheralded, the
'Directors' started appearing with names applied in the
usual Cowlairs transfers. It was fascinating keeping an
eye open for these, as it was not until some time later
than an official list of names was published which con-
firmed that they were a continuation of those carried by
the 'Scotts'. Full advantage was taken of the large
expanse of the splashers, which permitted magnificent
names like 'The Lady of the Lake', 'Lord James of
Douglas', and 'Wizard of the Moor'. 'Luckie Muckle-
backit', who I believe was a Newhaven fishwife, was in
charming contrast. Another change in these engines later
in the year was the removal of the deep valance on the
running plate, which facilitated oiling the coupling rods
and was more in keeping with contemporary fashions.
Countering the addition of 24 passenger engines to the
area was the withdrawal of fifteen North British 4-4-0s
from December 1922 - five Drummond Class D.27/8; three
'seven-footers', Class D.25; and the last seven
unrebuilt 'West Highland Bogies' Class D.35 as well as
three of Matthew Holmes' final 317 Class D.26.

Having only Saturday afternoons, two weeks holiday a
year, and the Edinburgh spring and autumn Monday holidays
available for photography was a very different situation
after one had been accustomed to long school holidays.
There could still be afternoon visits to Perth or
Stirling and even Pitlochry and Blair Atholl in the
family car, but Haymarket shed was useless owing to the

sun's position in the afternoon whilst Inverkeithing was
played out. The main thing was to find a location nearer
at hand, and fortunately we learned about Craigentinny
carriage sidings, which had become the meeting place of a
new group of railway enthusiasts and photographers -
indeed, the nucleus of the Scottish branch of the
Stephenson Locomotive Society. This was formed about
that year with my brother Douglas as first honorary
secretary.

Craigentinny carriage sidings, a mile or so south of
Waverley on the main line, was always full of life
between one o'clock and four o'clock on a Saturday afternoon especially at a time when weekend specials from the
country were very popular. As a result there were
always plenty of comings and goings.

Unlike many carriage sidings no special engines were
assigned for empty stock working to the main station, and
many trains arriving from the north or west of Waverley
continued to the sidings with their own train engines.
The same thing happened in the opposite direction when a
main line engine would arrive from the shed to take its
train up to the Waverley. Trains arriving at the east
end of the latter which required servicing at Craigentinny either came down with their own engines tender-
first or were hauled by a Haymarket engine coming to
collect its own north- or westbound train. Waverley
being a through station undoubtedly contributed to these
- to us - very convenient arrangements. Some engines
returned immediately to their shed, in the case of
Haymarket often taking up stock for the Berwick or
Carlisle lines, while others had their fires cleaned or
were generally serviced at the sidings, turning if
required en route to Waverley at the nearby triangle at
Abbeyhill. Thus in a very extensive carriage depot there
was only one shunter, J.83 0-6-0T No.9816.

All these empty stock movements provided a good
variety of subjects for the camera including practically
every N.B. type, even Atlantics, as well as the newcomers
which were to increase as the year went on. Freight
engines as well as shunting tanks were also plentiful as
they made their way home to St. Margaret's from the
marshalling yards at South Leith, Portobello and
Niddrie. It was altogether an ideal location when the
sun was shining. Moreover, fortunately the siding staff
and engine crews did not worry about our being there.

Photography was resumed again in April but with a new camera replacing my first 1A Junior Kodak, which in spite of the anastigmatic lens fitted in 1924 had been a little disappointing. Some of the fault did lie with commercial developing which often produced soft negatives quite unsuitable for our purpose. The new camera, of the same style as the Kodak, was a German-made Goerz Tenax with a good lens and a Compur shutter with speeds up to 1/350th of a second, quite suitable for fairly fast-moving subjects taken from reasonably far back. The size of the picture remained the same, $2\frac{1}{2}$" x $4\frac{1}{4}$". Two other improvements were changing to the French Pathe film and doing our own developing with a Kodak film tank which was the last word in the 1930s. In retrospect this certainly was a queer contraption, consisting of a wooden box with light-proof lid and a celluloid apron, also light-proof. By placing the film and apron in the tank, replacing the lid and turning two handles, the film and apron were interlaced on to a reel and, now completely safe, removed from the box and placed in the accompanying tank for normal time-and-temperature development. At last we had consistently good developing and were also able to make allowances for an entire film exposed in slightly poor conditions.

The five Glasgow-built Haymarket Pacifics had of course been followed without a break by the remaining fifteen (Nos.2568-82). These were fitted with the Westinghouse brake for work in the North Eastern Area, the first ten being shedded at Gateshead and the other five at Heaton, both Newcastle depots. It was extraordinary how dramatically the scene had changed at Haymarket in such a short time. Passing the shed on the way into Edinburgh in the mornings there were usually at the west end two Pacifics which had worked overnight trains from Newcastle and were awaiting their turn at the coaling stage. At the east end standing on the outgoing road were two more, having their drivers' final look round before moving on to the Waverley for the 10 a.m. 'Flying Scotsman' and 10.15 a.m. expresses. There were always several 'Directors' on view and practically every engine was turned out in apple green, whilst any still remaining in the old bronze green had been relettered L.N.E.R.

These new engines however were just a prelude, as in addition to the ex-R.O.D. Class 04 2-8-0s representatives

of yet another five English locomotive types were coming
to former North British territory during 1925. Most had
arrived by the middle of the year. An interesting
collection, they comprised: 25 J.9 ex-G.C. Parker
0-6-0s; fourteen K.2 ex-G.N. Gresley 2-6-0s; twelve N.2
Gresley 0-6-2Ts, newly built by Beyer Peacock; five K.3
Gresley 2-6-0s, part of a large batch of fifty being
built at Darlington; and fifteen D.1 ex-G.N. Ivatt
4-4-0s.

The Parkers all went to Parkhead, Kipps and other
sheds in the west to replace old Drummond and Wheatley
0-6-0s which were scrapped. The K.2s, which had had
their boiler mountings reduced similar to those already
in service on the Great Eastern area, were allocated
chiefly to Eastfield for later service on the West
Highland, but there were at least two at St. Margaret's
which were frequently seen in Fife. The N.2 0-6-2Ts went
to Eastfield, Dundee and St. Margaret's, replacing N.B.
4-4-2Ts on the inner local services, not immediately in
the case of those at St. Margaret's which at first shared
local goods duties with the humble ex-N.B. N.15 tank with
the same wheel arrangement. Later they were put on
regular service on the Edinburgh suburban trains. A
chimney 4" higher than their companions working from
Kings Cross on the Metropolitan lines altered their
appearance considerably and another change was to left-
hand drive. In an official Southern Scottish Area
classification of passenger engines their description was
given as 'Metropolitan Tank'. The N.2 certainly got off
the mark more quickly than the C.16 4-4-2Ts but were not
universally popular with their drivers.

The K.3 2-6-0s, divided between Eastfield and St.
Margaret's and only five in number, were a little out of
place as the North British, unlike the Caledonian, had
never favoured heavy mixed traffic engines with 5' 8"
driving wheels. Nevertheless from the enthusiasts' point
of view they were nice engines to have about and were
often seen on the Aberdeen road. Their North Eastern
style of cab with two side windows was certainly a great
improvement compared with the old Ivatt design. With low
boiler mountings necessary to comply with what was desig-
nated the new 'composite load gauge', they were very
different from the 1000 Class built by the Great Northern
Railway in 1920.

The D.1 was Ivatt's final design of 4-4-0 and all

fifteen of them came north, for no reason which seemed
apparent at the time or even subsequently! Cowlairs
appeared to have been at a loss as to what to do with
them and they received the already versatile N.B. classification 'M', being described as 'G.N. Type (3051)'
Class. It is interesting to note that the D.31 rebuilt
Holmes 4-4-0s which shared the same classification had
changed to 'M - second degree'. My first view of a D.1
was not encouraging. On the way home one evening we
passed a goods train climbing to Ferryhills with a green
engine banking. This in itself was unusual; moreover,
although we were travelling fast it was just possible to
see that the engine itself was something out of the
ordinary, so along to the railway I went. Soon there
were sounds of an engine approaching on the down line and
as it came through the road bridge at the central junction I saw No.3052 for the first time. Very strangely it
was making little 'peeping' sounds, due we discovered to
the cab roof which was vibrating shockingly, pulling on
the chain operating the whistle! Her driver, who was
treating his engine as a huge joke, told me she had been
sent to Dunfermline Upper to take her place with the
D.31s on the local passenger services, but apparently no
thought had been given to the fact that these were
composed of Westinghouse-fitted stock. The only alter-
native open to the shed foreman was to send No.3052 to
Inverkeithing, but she was not acceptable on banking
duties for very long and with the rest of the class was
subsequently fitted with the Westinghouse brake. The
D.1s spent much of their remaining lives acting as pilots
on the Aberdeen main line as well as to Newcastle in
company with North Eastern Atlantics. They were
certainly most interesting engines historically and did
compensate for D.31 4-4-0s which were going to the Great
North, the Northern Scottish Area.
     On a Saturday afternoon in April my brother and I had
a run to Perth to see how things were going on the L.M.S.
Our train, the 2.05 p.m. from Waverley, now upgraded to
vestibuled N.B. corridor stock with two Highland coaches
for Inverness, was a St. Margaret's turn and the engine
was 'Director' No.6389 'Haystoun of Bucklaw'. The
3.50 p.m. to Inverness went forward with No.14768 'Clan
Mackenzie', followed on the 'Blair Slow' by 'Ben-y-Gloe',
now No.14397. No.50B, the little Highland shunter, had
been to Lochgorm and had returned as a shining red

The most famous Pacific of all, No.4472 'Flying Scotsman', has just
arrived at Haymarket shed after turning on the Gorgie triangle, having
completed its non-stop run on the 'Flying Scotsman' in June 1928.

The important clearance test run of A.3 Pacific No.2573 'Harvester' on
Sunday 1 July 1928, photographed at Inverkeithing East Junction. Clearly
visible are the 'touch posts' on the chimney, cab ventilator edges and
cylinder covers.

The Royal Train at Ballater waiting to return empty to its home at Wolverton August 1928. Heywood 4-4-0 No.6850 'Hatton Castle', with the Royal Train headcode of four white discs, is coupled to a sister engine, No.6846 'Benachie'.

Paid off for the weekend at Blair Atholl shed on a summer Saturday evening in 1928 are four of Peter Drummond's 0-6-4Ts, used for many years on banking duties to Druimochdar summit.

The chairman of the L.N.E.R., William Whitelaw - without hat - standing in front of Gresley Pacific No.2563 'William Whitelaw' at a railway exhibition at Dunfermline in 1929. On his left is the Earl of Elgin, a director of the company, and on his right Major Stemp.

A unique combination of a 'Crab', No.13108, and a 'Strath', No.14274 'Strathcarron', leaving Aviemore in 1929 for Inverness on a long train of empty coaching stock including sleeping cars, destined for end-of-the-week southbound holiday traffic. This 'Strath' was withdrawn a week later.

Pacifics to Aberdeen at last. . . . A.3 No.2567 'Sir Visto', newly transferred to Dundee, passing North Queensferry on an Aberdeen - Kings Cross fish train, May 1930.

The north tower at North Queensferry, photographed from the summit of the centre cantilever, shows how lateral stability was achieved by the bases being much wider at the bottom than at the tops.

The huge vertical columns connected by similar crossed tubes at the centre of the Inchgarvie cantilever show to great advantage in this photograph taken from the footpath. Note, far above, the underside of the pathway along the top member.

A portion of the counterbalance weights can be seen in this photograph of the arch at the south end of Forth Bridge. On the right is the initial stairway to the cantilever towers - reversing one's direction at the cross girder was, to say the least, a little tricky. Left to right, W.D.M.Stephen, resident bridge inspector Bell.

Former L. & Y.R. rebuilt 4-6-0 No.10452 at Upperby shed, 1927. One of the earliest Horwich engines to carry the red livery, it had the letters L.M.S. on the cabside, and was one of a number which competed for a period with the 'Claughtons' between Crewe and Carlisle.

Standing at Durran Hill, the Midland shed at Carlisle, is No.999, the last of the two-cylinder 4-4-0s designed by R.M.Deeley as an experimental comparison with his better-known compound. They were mainly to be found north of Leeds on the 'Settle & Carlisle'.

One of the famous North Eastern Worsdell R Class 4-4-0s (L.N.E.R. D.20) built in 1899. Employed on express work between Carlisle and Newcastle, No.1235 was photographed at London Road shed.

N.B. Atlantic No.9905 'Buccleuch' at Canal shed. The name lost some of its impact, especially with its proximity to the large cab numerals, when its position was changed from the leading splashers to the second around 1928.

McIntosh's express goods 4-6-0 No.17906 at Kingmoor shed. His last
design for the Caledonian, this class of eleven engines did splendid work
over Beattock for many years.

0-6-0 No.12486 at Upperby shed, 1926. Formerly Maryport & Carlisle
Railway No.25, built by Beyer Peacock in 1878 and rebuilt in 1899, she
was scrapped in 1930. Note the deep buffer beam, which at one time had
accommodated a second set of buffers for the small colliery wagons in
the Maryport Dock area.

No.15012. The paint shop at Inverness certainly made a
beautiful job, notably of the black-and-yellow edging on
the curved corner of the cab front of the Jones engines.

There was very little else of fresh interest beyond a
selection of coaching stock transferred from the south to
the Highland. Some in their old livery, others in the
new, there were examples from the former L.N.W.R.,
Midland, and even the L. & Y., with those strangely
uncomfortable seat cushions covered with a material
resembling horsehair. We were a little shocked at seeing
a red-painted 'Castle' for the first time. In Highland
days the name was applied in two arcs positioned over the
leading pair of driving wheels. Now in a straight line
along the splasher the large name, 'Ballindalloch
Castle', looked for all the world like a station name-
board! This change was quite unexpected and greatly
resented by us at first.

At Perth South shed we were glad to see Pickersgill's
first three-cylindered 4-6-0 No.956, now painted red and
numbered 14800, which had arrived from Buchanan Street on
an Aberdeen express with a Dunalistair II as a pilot!
Otherwise, the shed included the usual collection of
Pickersgill and Dunalistair IV 4-4-0s and various mixed
traffic 4-6-0s.

The journey home was behind Atlantic No.901B 'St.
Johnstoun', which had worked north from Waverley on the
4.30 p.m., and at Dunfermline Lower we changed to a local
down to Inverkeithing with D.31 No.9640. It had been an
enjoyable day but unsuitable conditions for photography
had prevailed. Notable had been the few engines in pre-
Grouping colours.

Craigentinny's suitability for photography surpassed
all our expectations and I soon had photographs of the
K.3 and K.2 2-6-0s, the G.N. D.1s and the new N.2 0-6-2
tanks, as well as many of the N.B. types. There was also
plenty to see passing by and sometimes photograph, which
included stopping trains to and from Berwick, the
Waverley Route, Peebles, Dunbar and North Berwick, as
well as places nearer at hand like Musselburgh and
Penicuik. North Berwick and Dunbar still have a train
service while all the others have gone, and the Waverley
Route, alas, simply does not exist.

A never-to-be-forgotten little walk at Inverkeithing
took place about four o'clock one morning towards the end
of June when we made our way along a path, which is still

there, to the railway just north of the Jamestown
Viaduct. There we saw, going remarkably gently up the
hill, our old Great North friend No.45A with a train of
seven four-wheeled coaches, making its long journey to
Darlington for the 1924 Railway Centenary celebrations.
It was beautifully restored in the former Great North of
Scotland green, with its brass dome and other brass and
copper embellishments absolutely gleaming. Disappearing
into Ferryhills cutting, this was the last time I was to
see this little engine.

Our annual August holiday was at Strathpeffer, and
like Fort William in 1923 completely new ground for us;
in fact, we had never been north of Inverness before.
The most exciting prospect was the Kyle of Lochalsh line
and seeing a 'Skye Bogie' and also a 'Big Ben'! At that
time the latter were firmly wedded to the 'Farther
North'. There is always a thrill crossing the swing
bridge over the Caledonian Canal at Clachnaharry. Ahead
lies the upper reaches of the Beauly Firth, with beyond
the massive bulk of Ben Wyvis (3,429'), and it is easy to
understand how the magic words 'Farther North' came
about. Unfortunately from the railway point of view we
travelled by road. On the other hand, both road and rail
are close partners for much of the journey from Perth to
Inverness, and among many striking glimpses of the latter
was one of No.14388 'Loch Luichart' and No.14687 'Brahan
Castle' waiting in the heather in the very remote passing
place at Inchlea between Dalwhinnie and Newtonmore for a
northbound goods train, which we ourselves had overtaken
a few miles farther back.

Strathpeffer was the terminus of a short branch from
Fodderty Junction, three miles west of Dingwall on the
Kyle of Lochalsh route, which at the time of the opening
of the Strathpeffer branch in 1885 actually terminated at
Strome Ferry.

The rail link from Dingwall to the west coast, promoted by a company known as the Dingwall & Skye Railway and
opened in 1870, terminated as already stated at Strome
Ferry on the south shore of the narrow sea entrance to
Loch Carron. From there steamers sailed for Skye and the
Outer Hebrides, not altogether successfully. In 1880 the
Dingwall & Skye amalgamated with the Highland, which in
fact had always worked the line. Strome Ferry had never
been an ideal place for a harbour suitable for transfer
from rail to sea, and in 1897 the Highland Railway

extended the line to Kyle of Lochalsh, where they had
plenty of room to spread. This further ten miles made a
total distance from Dingwall of 63 miles.

Dingwall, 22 miles from Inverness, a large commercial
and farming centre as well as being the county town of
Ross-shire, had a four-platformed station, one of which
was an island and another the dock platform for the
Strathpeffer train. There was also an engine shed and
turntable dating back to 1870 and it was here that we had
our first view of a 'Skye Bogie'. Looking over the fence
on the main road into Dingwall from the south we saw
No.14277. We were soon over that fence and to our
surprise found a man crouching at the rear end of the
tender washing his hands with soap in a steady trickle of
water leaking from the tender. Driver McBean, who made
us very welcome, appeared to accept the state of his
engine's tender as nothing unusual. Nevertheless, before
we had finished our holiday No.14277 had a little trip to
Lochgorm Works, returning the next day with a tender
belonging to a sister, No.14282. She had a tremendous
cheer as she passed the shed leading 'Dunrobin Castle' on
the Wick 'mail', starting work immediately by disposing
of a couple of coaching vans which had been dropped by
the train it had just assisted - duly recorded by the
camera.

We discovered that there were three 'Skye Bogies' on
the Kyle of Lochalsh line: No.14277 at Dingwall, plus
No.33 (still in green) and No.14284 at 'the Kyle' - the
term normally used by the enginemen. Also at Dingwall
were 'Small Ben' No.14412 'Ben Avon' and two 4-4-0 tanks
(No.101 and No.15016), the former deputising for Drummond's 0-4-4 tank No.25 'Strathpeffer' which was
temporarily indisposed at Inverness. The other little
tank was a station and yard shunter.

'Ben Avon' was the Kyle 'mail' engine, her day
comprising an early morning trip to Inverness, then the
train of the day, to Kyle, returning in the late afternoon right through to Inverness and then finally home to
Dingwall with a late evening local. No.14277 worked a
forenoon goods to Kyle on certain days of the week,
otherwise acted as spare engine for the line. A 'Small
Ben' was allowed 170 tons and a 'Skye Bogie' 140 tons,
the main stumbling block being the long haul of 1 in 50
from Fodderty Junction to the Raven's Rock.

No.101 and her sister, No.102, had a most interesting

history. Originally built for a South American railway
(the Uruguay Eastern) which however did not accept them,
they were purchased by the Highland from their builders
Dubs & Co. of Glasgow in 1892. A builder's photograph
shows the first of the class complete with cow-catchers
and a vast headlamp, bearing the U.E.R. No.1 on the
chimney and the name 'Olmos'. The generously flared
brass chimney cap remained to the end of her days in 1934
as L.M.S. No.15013. A photograph of the second engine,
No.15014, as rebuilt by Drummond appears on page 85 of
'Scottish Steam in the 1920s'.

A forenoon at Dingwall usually started with a run on
the branch train leaving Strathpeffer about nine o'clock.
Closely following was the early morning train from Kyle,
a mixed passenger and goods with a 'Skye Bogie'. These
connected with a Tain - Inverness local hauled during the
time we were there by 'Big Ben' No.61 'Ben na Caillich'.
There was also a northbound Train local from Inverness
with another 'Big Ben'. The next train was the Wick
'mail' with connections from the south at Inverness,
invariably with No.14679 'Blair Castle', which brought a
through carriage from Inverness to Strathpeffer.

Following from Inverness was 'Ben Avon' on the Kyle
'mail', and completing a forenoon at Dingwall Junction a
run home, sometimes on the footplate, on the branch
train, which at the time consisted of a Highland six-
wheeler, an L.N.W. bogie composite, a Midland clerestory
six-wheeled guards brake and the through coach from
Inverness, another Midland clerestory. A day return
ticket also allowed travel on the Kyle line to Achterneed
station, which served and was named Strathpeffer before
the branch was opened.

Inevitably we had a day trip to Kyle, a beautiful and
comparatively level route except for the climb to Raven's
Rock, which was imposed upon the planners by local landowners who would not have a railway in Strathpeffer. But
for this the line would have generally followed the A832
to Garve. By the time the branch was proposed the
opposition had ceased.

From Garve the railway and road followed the same
route to the head of Loch Carron, the former taking the
south shore and the later (A890) the north to a point
opposite Strome Ferry where it ceased. This entailed a
ferry over to the south side, thence to Kyle of Lochalsh.
To enable motorists to avoid the ferry the Highland

Railway provided flat wagons for cars which could be
attached as required to any passenger trains between
Strathcarron and Kyle. They were also available at
Garve, which additionally relieved the motorist of some
forty miles of very bad road. They were still to be seen
there in 1939, surely one of the earliest examples of the
later 'motorail'. It is only in the last few years that
the A890 has been re-routed along the south bank of the
loch; closing the gap to Strome Ferry it constitutes a
very real threat to the existence of the railway. The
last few miles of the line into Kyle, twisting along the
shores of the loch with a view of the Cuillin Mountains
beyond, are very beautiful; finally the station is
reached, the railway's nearest point to the Isle of Skye.

Our run to Kyle on the last day of the holiday was a
fitting end to a holiday in the company of fascinating
engines we had never seen before.

Back in Edinburgh it was obvious that the naming of
the Gresley Pacifics was going ahead rapidly. No official notification of the names had appeared, and the first
three that came my way happened to be No.2572 'St.
Gatien', No.2574 'St. Frusquin' and No.2576 'The White
Knight', suggestive of a 'Knight' and 'Saint' Class.
However, a few days later No.2568 'Sceptre' was seen
waiting at Haymarket for the up 'Fish' and ere long we
learned that Gresley's Pacifics were going to bear the
names of racehorse winners.

I can remember very well thinking that the cast brass
nameplates were very austere compared with the colourful
gilt transfers used by the North British and Highland,
which somehow looked far more permanent and 'personal-
ised' - to use a term recently applied by British Rail to
the named Class 87 electrics on L.M. Region.

A most interesting railway year concluded with the
arrival in Scotland of a further six Class N.2 0-6-2
tanks (Nos.892-7). These were newly built at Doncaster
and fitted with Westinghouse brakes.

IX

THE GROUPING - 1926

Early in January 1926 the L.N.E.R. produced a new
locomotive design, a large 0-6-0 with 4' 8" driving
wheels intended for mineral service. Classed J.38, the
entire order of 35 engines was sent to Scotland and by
15 February No.1400 and No.1406 had arrived at Dunfermline Upper. I forget how many were stationed there
before the year was out but a photograph of the shed
taken from one of the lamp posts in June shows five
standing in the open, and almost certainly there were a
few more inside. The boiler was a completely new design.
Comparatively short - only 10' 9" between the tube
plates combined with a diameter of 5' 6" - it was somewhat ill-proportioned from the aesthetic point of view.
Designed at Darlington with, of course, a Doncaster style
of chimney, the J.38s were not works of art, although it
must be admitted that the essential dimensions were not
exactly promising material for the designer to work on.
They were however very powerful engines and were very
acceptable to the drivers in Fife. Later they were
followed by the well-known J.39, a similar design with
5' 2" wheels seldom seen north of the Border.

Another newcomer from Doncaster was the J.50 0-6-0
tank, a former Great Northern class. Seven of these were
eventually allocated to Eastfield where they took their
place with the N.15 0-6-2 tanks on shunting and short-
distance freights.

My photography started again this year in mid-March,
largely at Craigentinny but also at Leith Docks as well
as the large marshalling yard at South Leith. Both of
these were near the office and handy at lunchtime. The
Leith Dock Commission had no engines of their own,
shunting being in the hands of the ex-N.B. 0-4-0 saddle
tanks (Y.9) and the somewhat similar Caledonian 611 Class
built from 1895. For some reason or other there was also
an L. & Y. 0-4-0 saddle tank, a type which seemed to move
about the L.M.S. quite a lot over the years - finally to
the Keighley & Worth Valley Railway!

The fourth day of May 1926 was the first day of the
General Strike. At Inverkeithing station we were told
there would be a train into Edinburgh at 11.30 a.m. which

would return to Dundee at 1.08 p.m. All going well there
would be two more trains, a 2.15 p.m. from Waverley to
Dundee returning late in the evening.

Having phoned the office I was told to get a volunteer
job, so next day proceeded to Dunfermline Upper with a
companion similarly marooned. The position there was
that only one driver had reported for work and in fact he
had already started a very long day with a volunteer
fireman. We were both taken on as firemen, my companion
on the day shift and myself from 10 p.m. to 6 a.m. Apart
from the hope that more drivers might appear, three
engines were kept in steam in addition to the one that
was out. The shed foreman attended the shed in the daytime and there was always one of his assistants present,
strictly in an advisory capacity, who would nevertheless
have taken an engine out on the line in the event of some
real emergency. Sleeping accommodation was provided in
two corridor coaches supplied with pillows and rugs as it
was considered inadvisable to leave the shed premises.
As far as I can remember food largely came out of tins
supplemented by the usual eggs, bacon and sausages, all
brought in by the foremen. There were four engines in
steam: D.32 No.9893, one of Reid's 'Small Intermediates'
- with 6' driving wheels and a superheater, she was well
ahead of the normal run of passenger engines at the depot
and had been sent there temporarily with the possible
emergency in view; two other 4-4-0s, D.31s No.9640 and
No.9262; whilst J.36 0-6-0 No.628B 'Byng' completed the
four. Night duty consisted of looking after the inject-
ors and putting a shovelful of coal in the fireboxes from
time to time, the latter too enthusiastically one night
when No.9262's safety valves started 'lifting'. The
foreman soon put things right, muttering that there 'was
enough steam to take her to Stirling and back' and adding
'let her alone noo'. On the eighth day, no more drivers
having reported, it was decided to keep only No.9893 and
No.9262 in steam. Night duty became a greater farce than
ever and my afternoons were devoted to doing a bit of
cleaning, something I had always wanted to do. Cleaning
No.9893's firebox and smokebox after it had spent a long
day at places as far apart as Anstruther on the Fife
coast and Perth and Edinburgh was a ghastly experience
the first time, especially the smokebox - which to me was
a shambles. On Wednesday 12 May the General Strike was
called off, and my short stay at Dunfermline Upper ended.

The following day there were quite a few trains running, including a remarkable one from Edinburgh to
Aberdeen and back which stopped at all stations. This
was headed by superheated 'Scott' No.9428 'Adam
Woodcock'. By Monday 17 June we knew the immediate
pattern of the future train service, severely curtailed
by the coal strike which was in fact going to drag on for
months. Affecting me personally was no evening train
home between 5.35 and 7.55 p.m. Then as time passed
coal was imported and train services improved.

Saturday 5 June was the occasion of a Scottish Branch
S.L.S. afternoon visit to Stirling. It was an absolutely
perfect day and our first call was at the former Caledonian shed where I took photographs of Pickersgill and
McIntosh small-wheeled 4-6-0s for the Oban line,
Dunalistair II 4-4-0s, and very fortunately Drummond
4-4-0 No.1070, still in blue livery and rebuilt with a
Dunalistair I boiler. There were a lot of engines laid
up due to the coal strike including No.14309, one of
Drummond's first express engines built in 1866; also, a
small-wheeled version for the Greenock line, No.1114,
which followed in 1891. Both had long ropes for the slip
coupling dangling from their boiler handrails, being on
the last lap on banking duties between Stirling and
Dunblane. Also as a result of the emergency the Killin
branch was closed, and standing together were the branch
engine, Drummond 0-4-4 tank No.15103, and allocated as
her understudy a similar engine (No.1175) in very faded
blue.

A welcome visitor was an ex-G. & S.W.R. Peter Drummond
large 2-6-0 which was a very tight fit on the turntable
and had temporarily put the latter out of commission;
not that it mattered unduly as there was very little
movement at the shed that afternoon beyond engines being
shifted for our benefit by a very helpful shed staff.
On the L.N.E.R. at the Forth and Clyde shed were a
'seven-footer', No.594B, and G.7 Holmes 0-4-4 tank
No.9591. The latter and a G.9 Reid 0-4-4 tank No.9474,
photographed at the main line shed, were most welcome as
the advent of the N.2 0-6-2 tanks had tended to move
these engines away from the Edinburgh district. Stirling
was one of the earliest Scottish S.L.S. visits and it
will be remembered very happily by those who were there..

Not so successful was a visit to Carstairs by seven
members on 3 July. Again it was a nice day but the shed,

alas, was one of those which ran east and west, with the
sun completely end-on. We were fortunate to get two
photographs of old Caledonian and G. & S.W.R. 4-4-0s at
the right angle on the turntable, after which we remained
on the station platform watching the trains pass.

Looking up the line we suddenly spied a very new Derby
compound slowly rounding the spur from the Edinburgh line
to the signal box at Strawfrank Junction on the main
line, where it stopped to await a train for the south.
Regrettably, with the exception of one member who had
more discretion, we dropped our raincoats and charged up
the main line, regardless of anything else other than
getting a photograph. No.1066, which was standing perf-
ectly posed in full sunlight, was equipped for burning
oil fuel, an added bonus. To our great surprise we had
no reprimands from the station staff when we rejoined our
companion.

August 1926 found us once more at Strathpeffer. Again
travelling by road we left home on the Friday evening
going via Aberdeen, where we stayed the night with relatives. Continuing next morning there was time for a quick
look round Kittybrewster. The biggest change from the
last visit in 1924 was that all the engines were painted
apple green apart, of course, from the three tank engine
classes. There were numerous idle engines about due to
the coal crisis, including several D.31 4-4-0s transferred from the Southern Scottish Area. In less than
half an hour I had secured twenty first-class negatives.
Most interesting was one of 'Sir David Stewart' half-
suspended by the sheerlegs and resting on wooden blocks
in place of the bogie, which presumably had been removed
to allow sufficient tilt to roll out the rear drivers.

There were a few changes at Dingwall. 'Ben Avon' was
still on the Kyle 'mail' together with No.14277. Kyle
also had No.14284 and No.33, now a shining red No.14283.
With the copper rim on its original chimney brightly
polished and white-painted cylinder ends it was a real
picture. In addition Kyle had another 'Skye Bogie',
No.14279.

The two little tank engines of 1925 had now been
replaced by two of Stroudley's three 0-6-0 tanks built
between 1869 and 1874. No.16118, which had been fitted
with larger side tanks and named 'Dornoch' when she was
sent to the Dornoch branch in 1902, was deputising for a
few days for the branch engine, 0-4-4T No.25 'Strath-

peffer' which, however, did return to her duties before
our holiday was over. No.57B 'Lochgorm', still in green,
was yard and station shunter.

The only other change worthy of comment was the withdrawal due to the coal situation of the 'Farther North
Express', which provided a fast service between Inverness
and Wick on Fridays and had resumed running in 1925.
Leaving Inverness at 4.30 p.m. in pre-war days its first
stop was at The Mound, more than half of the 162-mile
journey, but I have no record of its post-war scheduled
stops. At any rate, when I saw it, its 'Small Ben'
No.14411 'Ben Loyal' had a bogie tender carrying 200
gallons more water than the normal six-wheeled type.

My brother had travelled north by train, and choosing
the old route via Forres saw there, just for a moment,
what at first sight looked like a 'Skye Bogie' although
the splashers appeared on the large side. His thoughts
turned to the old 'Duke' Class, but according to our very
scanty records we had seen the last of these, 'Atholl'
and 'Dochfour', at Aviemore two years previously. Our
driver friends at Dingwall had no constructive suggest-
ions, quite convinced that it could not be a 'Skye Bogie'
as there were not enough to spare for 'places like
Forres'.

It was only fifty miles to Forres, so we decided to
call en route at Inverness shed. Many photographs have
been taken on the turntable at Inverness roundhouse,
which had 24 bays and was completed in 1864. Apart from
a larger turntable there had been few changes. Very
striking was the arch which spanned the approach road a
short distance from the turntable. Monumental in conception and almost giving an impression of guarding the
shed, it had a water tank concealed by its elaborate
stonework.

The shed foreman, fortunately, allowed us to look
round and take photographs. At home were two 'Clans',
three 'Castles', one 'Big' and three 'Small Bens', three
'Lochs', No.89A 'Sir George', one of the few remaining
'Straths', three Jones goods 4-6-0s and three 'Barney'
0-6-0s. Representing tank engine classes there was one
0-6-4T, two of the Drummond outside-cylindered 0-6-0Ts
built from spare parts (referred to in an earlier chapter) and - particularly interesting - No.16415, a new
L.M.S. 0-6-0 tank ('Jinty' in later years). With another
at Forres these made up the first newcomers to the

Highland apart from Caledonian infiltration from Perth as
far as Blair Atholl. No.16415 contrasted splendidly with
No.16383, the third of Stroudley's 0-6-0 tanks which we
were seeing for the first time. It is interesting how
these three Stroudley tanks differed in small details.
None of the chimneys for instance were the same, and
whereas all the driving wheels on No.16383 and No.16118
were solid the leading and trailing drivers on 'Lochgorm'
were spoked. 'Lochgorm', as No.16119, ended her days in
1934 with No.16383's chimney and probably her boiler as
well. Recently withdrawn and looking very neglected in a
siding was 'Skye Bogie' No.88A, too late to get a red
coat and the No.14281 allotted to her. Last year she had
been Inverness station shunter.

Inverness station we found almost impossible from the
photographic angle. Built at various times, its unusual
planning is well known. Viewed from the circulating area
and buffer stops the layout was V-shaped, with the right
arm for southbound traffic and the left for trains to the
north and west. A short distance from the platform ends
both lines joined a loop running from south to north,
thus forming a triangle inside which was sited Lochgorm
Works. It was therefore possible for traffic to and from
the north to bypass the station.

It was customary for trains from the south to use this
loop as far as the junction at the north end of the
triangle, there reversing into one of the north platforms
which was very convenient for passengers joining trains
for Wick or Kyle standing nearby, and at the same time
releasing the engine at once. Similarly trains from the
north backed into the south platforms alongside one bound
for Perth and the south.

Traffic has decreased considerably and if plans to
demolish the north section of the station are passed,
then trains for the north and west will also have to be
propelled from the south platforms before reversing and
continuing their journeys. It will be a pity as Inverness station, as it has been for so many years, still
retains a pleasant old world atmosphere.

Whether by road or rail it is a nice run from
Inverness to Forres, rewarded by magnificent views across
the Moray Firth to the mountains of Sutherland. Immediately we arrived at Forres shed our mystery was solved.
No.14278, numbered among the 'Skye Bogies', was one of
the 'Duke' Class and examination of the motion revealed

the number 82A, which had lost its name 'Durn' to
Cumming's new 4-4-0 in 1916. It was extraordinary how
this one engine had survived and looking back how ill-
informed we railway enthusiasts were at that time. I
took a nice photograph of No.14278, which was going to
soldier on for another four years.

Other engines at the shed were No.4 'Ben More',
No.14415 'Ben Bhach Ard' (both 'Small Bens') and two more
of the few remaining 'Straths', No.14275 'Glentruim' and
No.14276 'Glenbruar'. A couple of 'Barneys' and the
second 'Jinty', whose number I have forgotten, completed
the engines on display.

Forres was the point where the original main line to
the south parted company with the eastbound line to Elgin
and Keith. The station was built on a triangle and at
the time of our visit had up and down platforms on both
the Perth and Keith lines as well as a single platform
for any trains likely to travel directly between south
and east. With platforms on each arm of the triangle it
was quite an imposing station but it has of course been
greatly reduced in size with the closure of the Forres -
Aviemore section.

Elgin, ten miles farther east, was served by both the
L.M.S. and L.N.E.R., each with its own station. The
former, a simple two-platform country station, lay to the
west of the town. Both were connected by a spur used by
through traffic between the lines of the former Highland
and Great Northern Railways. Completely reconstructed in
1902 the L.N.E.R. station had impressive buildings in the
Scottish style and ample platform roofing, with one very
long platform for the few through trains between Aberdeen
and Inverness. This had an extension to the L.M.S.
station. At the east end were three dock platforms used
by Lossiemouth trains as well as those for the south via
the coast through Buckie and other ports on the Moray
Firth. Eventually at Cairnie Junction (48 miles from
Aberdeen) the latter rejoined the main line from Elgin
via Craigellachie, which was the shorter route to Aberdeen by six miles. Very little to it, it was
nevertheless the 'main line'. The station was very well
planned and it was possible for trains to and from the
coast and Lossiemouth to use the three bays without
interfering with any movement on the main line.

Elgin shed was very quiet. Standing in the yard were
three D.41 Johnson or Pickersgill 4-4-0s and D.42

No.6810, a rebuilt Manson which was working the branch to
Lossiemouth. Waiting to take the lunch car express from
Inverness to Aberdeen was brightly polished D.38 No.6877,
one of the three Manson engines built with 6' 6½" driving
wheels and since superheated. This train, of ex-Great
North vestibuled stock, and one of the little North
Eastern restaurant cars hired successively in the past by
the N.B. and G.N. stopped in the L.M.S. station where
No.6877 took over from No.14414 'Ben Udlaman'. Continuing to the L.N.E.R. station it waited there five minutes
before resuming its journey via Craigellachie to
Aberdeen. A curious anomaly was that the distance from
Elgin to Keith was eighteen miles compared with 27 via
Craigellachie. Most of the former Great North system has
disappeared and the only passenger trains today are the
fast d.m.u. services between Aberdeen and Inverness;
seven in each direction, daily except on Sundays, these
take the former L.M.S. route from Keith to Elgin!

Before we left Strathpeffer for home we had a look at
the 13½-mile branch line from Muir of Ord Junction to
Fortrose on the Black Isle, the long peninsula separating
the Cromarty Firth and the Inverness Firth. On duty was
another 'Skye Bogie', No.87A, which driver Porter posed
very handily for us on the turntable. We were sorry to
learn that she was due for withdrawal at any time;
indeed, according to official records this happened only
two weeks after our visit.

The second year at Strathpeffer had been a success and
one of the highlights was lying on a grass slope at
Fodderty Junction watching the little Stroudley tank
No.16118, with its rapidly revolving 3' 7" drivers,
dashing along on the Strathpeffer branch services.

This occasion I returned home by train, leaving Dingwall at 8 a.m. behind 'Ben Avon', continuing from
Inverness behind No.14684 'Duncraig Castle' and No.14762
'Clan Campbell'. We were very late at Perth due to
'crossing' problems and missed the usual connection
there, so continued to Edinburgh as a special. I see
from my diary that I remained on the train to Edinburgh
instead of changing at Dunfermline Lower, probably to
experience the unusual joy of passing Inverkeithing non-
stop.

The only other item of exceptional interest which I
can recall before 1926 ended was the appearance at
Haymarket of a Great Eastern Holden 4-6-0 (No.8526) which

was en route for testing on the River Spey bridge at
Craigellachie. Although the Great North was urgently
requiring more powerful engines several years had to pass
before Stratford could afford to part with any of their
4-6-0s.

The coal situation had greatly affected passenger and
freight services but nevertheless it had been an interesting year and photographically quite successful. 1926
also marked the end of the pre-Grouping engine and coach
liveries as far as my observations extended. Very
noticeable was the increase in compartment stock
transferred from the North Eastern Area and the consequ-
uent phasing out of the more elderly N.B. carriages - a
much needed improvement for travellers.

X
THE GROUPING - 1927

Although many of the photographs taken with the Goerz camera had been quite satisfactory it was clear that a faster speed than 1/350th second was desirable. As a result we invested in a quarter-plate Relfex with a negative size of 3¼" x 4¼". The cheapest other offering was a Houghton Butcher 'Popular Pressman' with a roller blind shutter with three fixed slits, the smallest being very narrow indeed. The extent to which the shutter was wound selected which slit passed the lens, whilst adjusting a tension screw provided speeds ranging from one second to 1/1000th second. Very large lens were just coming to the fore at the time so we fell for the least expensive, an 'Aldis' f3.5. Even stopping down to f11 failed to give satisfactory definition so the camera was exchanged for another of the same make with a Ross 'Express' f4.5, a lens which ranked with the best in the world. It was a very heavy and bulky camera and vibrated shockingly when the shutter was released, so that at any speed below 1/150th second a tripod was necessary. Made of wood and telescopic of course, this in itself was no lightweight; the whole outfit, in a heavy leather case together with up to two dozen loaded dark slides, was quite a lot to contend with. Nevertheless it was transported to the top of the Forth Bridge cantilever towers, has been to the coal face in the Aitken pit at Kelty (where flash pictures were taken with a bit of touch paper leading to a pile of magnesium powder on a biscuit tin lid!) as well as many miles over the Cairngorm Mountains. With experience it became quite easy on shed visits to chase a moving engine, camera and tripod under one arm, frantically signalling to the driver with the other to please stop. Moreover it became only a matter of seconds to set the tripod and camera correctly to take a photograph.

Our first plates were orthochromatic, which could be developed in a dark room with a faint red light. Panchromatic, which came along later, necessarily had to be processed in total darkness, and for this we had a small tank with a rack into which were loaded six plates in pairs, negative side outwards, to ensure contact with the

developing solution. The rack was then inserted in the
light-proof tank for time and temperature development.
Loading dark slides with plates also required great care
and one had to know exactly where everything was in the
darkroom. If things became confused as they sometimes
did it was really quite easy to establish which was the
negative slide by moistening the teeth and gently biting
one corner of the plate and feeling the emulsion. Even
the best of us experienced moments of panic when a corner
of a plate was completely bitten off in this way.

Plate, like film material, was very slow, and a
favourite speed for stationary subjects was 350 H. & D.
The fastest we could get for moving trains was 700 H. &
D., both by Ilford.

Another step forward was securing a permit to take
photographs at any time at Haymarket, St. Margaret's and
Eastfield sheds and also from the entrances to The Mound
and Calton tunnels at the Waverley. I seldom had the
courage to take advantage of the latter two facilities.

Returning to current events on the railway, very few
engines were built for the L.N.E.R. during 1927, the most
interesting from the northerners' point of view being
twenty N.7 0-6-2 tanks, a development of the Stratford
design fitted with condensing gear for working in the
Kings Cross orbit. Built by Beardmores at Dalmuir on the
Clyde they were delivered between July and September,
and over this period two could be seen at Eastfield shed
on any Saturday afternoon newly delivered from the
builders.

Eastfield was by far the largest running shed on the
former North British and on a Saturday afternoon, with
the addition of engines coming home for the weekend as
well as those overhauled at Cowlairs Works and awaiting
return to their home sheds, it was a photographer's
paradise. With the added bonus of engines waiting to
enter Cowlairs sometimes for scrapping it must at one
time or another been host to any and every type of engine
on the Southern Scottish Area. We certainly always
seemed to strike oil on our Saturday afternoon visits,
one glorious occasion finding two freshly-painted Atlantics standing in the open. An odd little pair at
Eastfield were the dainty little J.71 six-coupled tanks,
No.285 and No.453 of North British origin, which had been
transferred from Carlisle in 1927. Chiefly engaged in
shifting dead engines to and from Cowlairs Works, they

remained at Eastfield until withdrawn in 1926 and 1939
respectively.

The success in the London area of the N.7 0-6-2Ts, of
which large numbers had been built in the preceding few
years, had resulted in further transfers from over the
Border, and August saw the first arrival in Scotland of a
batch of twenty N.2 0-6-2 tanks. These were Nos.4721-40
which had been built by the North British Locomotive Co.
in 1920. Stripped of their condensing gear and still
with the lower chimney associated with the Metropolitan
lines, they were probably the comeliest of the various
styles of these engines. Among the sheds they were
allocated to were Dunfermline Upper and North Berwick.

Other newcomers were the vanguard of twenty little
J.69 tanks built for the Great Eastern Railway by Holden
1890-1904, which were eventually to be found as far apart
as St. Margaret's in the south, Eastfield in the west,
and Kittybrewster in the north. No.7089 distinguished
itself as L.N.E.R. station pilot at Perth for nearly
fourteen years. Complete with Stratford stovepipe chimneys - unlike those left behind which were being fitted
with cast funnels after the North Eastern style - they
were a picturesque addition to our part of the world, and
it is difficult to realise now that at that time few of
us had seen many Great Eastern engines, and here they
were on our own doorstep!

In mid-summer the S.L.S. had a very successful day at
Kilmarnock. The first call was at the works and among
the various G. & S.W.R. types under repair were two
Highland 'Small Bens' (one being No.14400 'Ben More')
which were being rebuilt with new boilers. Hurlford
shed, comparatively near the works, naturally had a lot
on view and very well represented were Manson designs,
passenger and goods, both rebuilt by Whitelegg and in the
original style. There were also several rebuilt Smellie
engines as well as Stirling 4-4-0s of the 1870s which
were still busy on local trains. Unfortunately neither
'Baltics' nor Manson 4-6-0s made an appearance. It was
an excellent day for photography and fully justified the
long journey.

August found us once more staying at Strathpeffer.
'Ben Avon' still performed on the 'mail' and our old
friend No.14277 was still at Dingwall. Yet again the two
tank engines had been changed. No.25 'Strathpeffer' -
probably No.15051 by this time - was absent as usual;

one felt that she had an annual service every August;
and deputising for her on the Strathpeffer branch was
4-4-0T No.15014, the second of the engines built for
South America and as stated earlier rebuilt by Drummond.
Station and yard shunter was 0-4-4T No.15050, built by
Jones as a saddle tank in 1890 and rebuilt eleven years
later by Drummond with side tanks. This had carried two
names in its time: 'Strathpeffer' when on the Strathpeffer branch and 'Lybster' for later service on the Wick
and Lybster branch. This latter name was carried until
she was turned out in L.M.S. red.

Kyle had four 'Skye Bogies', No.14282, No.14284,
No.14279 plus a newcomer, No.14285 (formerly H.R. No.48
and the last of the class, built in 1901).

As far as we could foresee this was to be our last
holiday at Strathpeffer, which the family felt had been
fully exploited. From the railway point of view the
visits had just been in time to see the 'Skye Bogies'
almost completely in charge of their own territory;
indeed 'Ben Avon' had been the only intruder, a situation
due almost entirely to the numbers of 'Small Bens' and
'Lochs' withdrawn for re-boilering in the years 1926-29.
Including visits to Inverness we had met all the Highland
tank engines extant in the 1920s. Their grand total of
27 engines was represented by as many as seven different
classes, all very different and extremely attractive. We
had good times at Dingwall and were sorry to say goodbye
to the drivers and their mates who had helped us so much.

Passenger trains to Strathpeffer ceased in 1946 and
the branch was closed in 1952. Before the First World
War, in order to attract holidaymakers to their luxurious
new hotel at Strathpeffer Spa, the Highland Railway
provided a connection at Aviemore with the 11.50 a.m.
from Perth. Known in the timetable as the 'Strathpeffer
Spa Express', by using the through loop at Inverness it
ran non-stop from Aviemore to Dingwall where it changed
engines for the branch. There is an official photograph
of this train headed by No.129 'Loch Maree', proudly
bearing the headboard 'Strathpeffer Spa'.

Back in Edinburgh our thoughts centred on the coming
'Royal Scots' for the L.M.S. As is well known, an urgent
order had been placed for fifty to be built by the North
British Locomotive Co. in 1927, and rumour had it that
the first should appear by September and also that five
were destined for Polmadie. A slow train from Glasgow

(Central) arriving at Princes Street station about 7.45
a.m. was a favourite roster for running in new or freshly
repaired engines, and sure enough this became a 'Royal
Scot' working. Photography at Princes Street was difficult at the best of times and at that early hour almost
an impossibility, so the solution seemed to lie at
Murrayfield Junction where we had seen our first red
Caledonian engine turning on the triangle. To be there
before eight o'clock in the morning yet be at the office
in Leith by nine was quite an expedition, but it was
successful. Thanks to expertise with the tripod and
camera - as there was no question here of the driver
waiting for us - a satisfactory photograph of No.6127 was
obtained which certainly deserves a place in this volume
of memories. The early morning sun is quite evident.

The 'Royal Scots' were a tremendous boost to the
morale of the L.M.S. supporters in Edinburgh. Undoubtedly magnificent-looking machines with the very excellent
finish always associated with the N.B.L. Co., they were
very fitting subjects on which to end the year's
photography.

XI

THE GROUPING - 1928

One can say that 1928 was an exceptionally good year
in Scotland for the railway enthusiast. On the L.N.E.R.
there was the advent of the new D.49 three-cylinder
4-4-0s and the introduction of non-stop running between
Kings Cross and Waverley, while on the L.M.S. the new
'Royal Scots' were getting into their stride on the West
Coast Route and Derby compounds were monopolising the
express services on former Caledonian and Glasgow & South
Western lines.

Named after counties served by the L.N.E.R. the new
D.49s were publicised as the 'Shire' Class, the first
order from Darlington Works being for 28, fifteen of
which were destined for Scotland. Of these fourteen had
piston valves with Gresley valve gear - D.49/1 - and one
with (oscillating) cam-operated Lentz poppet valves -
D.49/3. (D.49/2 comprised two engines with differently
operated Lentz poppet valves, the forerunners of the
'Hunt' Class introduced several years later for the North
Eastern Area.)

England had seen the first of the 'Shires' towards the
end of 1927 but it was not until January following that
they made their debut farther north, the first I saw
being No.264 'Stirlingshire'. Fortunately she was on a
slow from Queen Street which frequently ran beside our
morning train to Edinburgh on the quadrupled track
between Saughton Junction and Waverley, so there was
plenty of time to study her at the buffer stops of
Platform Thirteen.

With raised running plate, smokebox, and front end
almost identical with the B.16 mixed traffic 4-6-0s, it
was obvious that Darlington had been allowed a lot of
scope in the designing. The short J.39 boiler was not an
asset either, and the general appearance was just a
little disappointing, particularly - and not for the
first time - the Doncaster chimney. Some of our feelings
were undoubtedly due to the fact that we had anticipated
a true Gresley engine. The chimney brings to mind a
comment in the 'Railway Magazine' for May 1938 in an
illustrated description of the first B.16 to be fitted
with Gresley/Walschaerts valve gear.

In this the writer, contending that the rebuilt
No.2364 had undeniable claims to being the most handsome
mixed traffic engine on British railways, questioned how
far its appearance would be altered with a Gresley
chimney instead of the North Eastern pattern fitted.
This, shortened for the composite loading gauge, was very
stylish indeed. To me the Doncaster chimney should have
ended when the side windowed cab was adopted as standard
but perhaps Great Northern fans think otherwise. Nevertheless it was thrilling to have a three-cylinder 4-4-0
on the Southern Scottish Area, and watching them climbing
the 1 in 70 to Ferryhills was something worthwhile.
    The Scottish 'Shires' were allocated as follows:
Haymarket, two; St. Margaret's, five; and Dundee, six;
with another two at Perth - appropriately, these were
No.250 'Perthshire' and later on No.329 'Inverness-
shire'. The former took us to the office every morning
in turn with 'Directors' No.6387 'Lucy Ashton' and
No.6388 'Captain Craigengelt'. The 'Shires' developed a
bad name for rough riding as they grew older, but it is
nice to recall the days when the two senior Perth drivers
described them as 'grand engines' which they never
seemed to cease polishing.
    In May my brother and I had a permit to visit the
L.M.S. shed at Polmadie in Glasgow. Fortunately the
weather was kind and I obtained some good photographs of
the new 'Royal Scots' stationed there, Nos.6127-32.
Beautifully kept, they had no names at that time, only
mounts ready for nameplates in the future. What these
were to be we did not know at the time.
    An S.L.S. visit to the other main L.M.S. Glasgow shed,
Balornock, later in the summer - primarily to photograph
the Caley 'single' - was a bitter disappointment. She
was specially moved into the open for us but like Carstairs the sun was absolutely end-on and moreover shining
on the tender end. No move was made to pose No.14010, in
red livery, on the turntable and a photograph was out of
the question.
    The first of May in 1928 was a big day on the L.N.E.R.
with the inauguration of the non-stop up and down 'Flying
Scotsman' made possible by the provision of Gresley's
corridor tenders, of which ten had been ordered. Haymarket shed was temporarily allocated No.2573 'Harvester'
and No.2580 'Shotover' for this service, both from the
North Eastern Area.

Unfortunately I was unable to see the departure of the
first up train with 'Shotover', in charge of Haymarket
driver Tom Henderson with driver J. Day of Kings Cross
taking over.   There was however a large crowd of people
to see the arrival of the down train with No.4472 'Flying
Scotsman', which had the well-known Gateshead driver Tom
Blades at the regulator.   We were all very suitably
impressed when we saw the equally celebrated top link
Kings Cross driver Albert Pibworth leaving the front
coach with his fireman and having a chat with their
co-enginemen in No.4472 before she puffed gently away to
Haymarket shed after her 392.7 mile run, successfully
completed.   The old frontiers were fast disappearing.
Although 'Flying Scotsman' had developed a hot tender
axlebox on her first journey she was able to complete the
round trip on next day's non-stop, to be replaced temporarily by No.2546 'Donovan'.   Quite historical now is the
North British style engine headboard produced for their
first run by Haymarket shed bearing the words 'Flying
Scotsman' in black letters on a white ground.   Kings
Cross followed suit immediately and spreading to other
L.N.E.R.-named trains these boards in different form
finally became universal on Britain's railways.
    Haymarket shed on a mid-summer evening we found to be
very suitable for photography and I got some nice photographs of the non-stop Pacifics, especially posed for me
by the engine shifter Ross Dougan.   He was well-known in
later years as a very well-liked assistant foreman at
Haymarket shed.
    The Reid Atlantic was still of course the premier
express engine on the Southern Scottish Area and their
loadings make interesting comparisons with the 'Shires':

	C.11	D.49
Edinburgh - Carlisle	290 tons	250 tons
Edinburgh - Berwick	380 tons	350 tons
Edinburgh - Aberdeen	370 tons	340 tons
Edinburgh - Perth	325 tons	300 tons
Edinburgh - Glasgow	410 tons	390 tons

    The ultimate aim of course was to use Gresley Pacifics
throughout from Kings Cross to Aberdeen, and on Sunday
1 July 1928 A.3 Pacific No.2573 'Harvester' made a
clearance trial run to Montrose.   I was able to get a
record of her passing Inverkeithing East Junction coupled
to the former N.B. directors' saloon.   'Touch posts' were

fitted to the chimney, cab ventilator and cylinder edges. This trial had been preceded earlier in the year when the four-span Jamestown Viaduct at Inverkeithing was thoroughly tested. With No.2563 'William Whitelaw' standing on the up line in various locations, No.2567 'Sir Visto' with a saloon attached to steady the tender passed over the bridge on the down line at varying speeds. Some of these, taking full advantage of the 1 in 70 downgrade, were very fast indeed - and were enjoyed on the footplate by my two brothers and I. The small bow spring girder bridge a little to the north, known as the Old Manse Bridge, was similarly tested on another Sunday. It was not however until the middle of 1930 that the Atlantics surrendered to the Pacific.

In August we returned once more to Ballater, our first visit since 1914. Apart from the engine and coach liveries plus the presence of a few rebuilt Holmes 4-4-0s little had changed. Fortunately we were there when the Royal Train arrived, hauled by Heywood 4-4-0s No.6850 'Hatton Castle' and No.6846 'Benachie', with King George V and Queen Mary en route to Balmoral. The train remained only sufficiently long for the drivers to look round their engines, and with little spare time available - and no inclination on the part of the drivers to pose their engines - it was possible to get only one exposure at the shed. It was possible however to get a photograph of the entire train waiting at the platform to proceed to Aberdeen and then home to Wolverton.

My only glimpses in 1928 of the Highland were at Perth and on a Saturday afternoon at Blair Atholl. The latter resulted in a rare picture of the four 0-6-4 banking tanks standing in a row waiting to resume their work on Monday after the weekend.

During the course of the year we made several visits to Eastfield, but even there with all the variety it was beginning to pall a little, and it was decided that to take full advantage of the Reflex next year would be devoted largely to photographs of moving trains.

43

XII
THE GROUPING - 1929-30

Early in 1929 Gresley Pacifics commenced regular
running on the Waverley Route with the allocation to
Canal shed at Carlisle of three newly-constructed high
pressure A.3 Pacifics, No.2745 'Captain Cuttle', No.2748
'Colorado', and No.2749 'Flamingo'. Consequently the
Atlantics were displaced from all the more important
trains to and from the old Midland line to Leeds and St.
Pancras. Canal shed was very proud of their Pacifics,
which were a pleasure to look at, and it is interesting
to record that 'Flamingo' remained there from her first
arrival in February 1929 until withdrawn in April 1961.

Another eight new 'Shires' were also added to L.N.E.R.
locomotive stock. Numbered 2753-60, seven went to Eastfield (largely replacing the 'Directors' on the Edinburgh
- Glasgow main line) and one to St. Margaret's. For
several months No.2753 'Cheshire' worked from Perth
pending the results of tests on the temperamental D.49/3
'Inverness-shire' which were being conducted from
Eastfield shed.

On a visit to Perth we found considerable changes, not
least on the Highland Division which had recently been
presented with ten Horwich 'Crab' 2-6-0s as well as the
six 'River' Class. Combined with the eight 'Clans' the
Highland authorities were really well off, and this
situation was to improve even further when the Stanier
'Black Fives' took over. The 'Crabs' then retired
farther south; the 'Clans' went to the Oban line, where
after distinguished work they too were displaced by the
Stanier invaders. The 'Rivers' however remained on the
line they were originally intended for.

One Sunday afternoon at Perth North shed there was an
imposing display of engine power with three 'Clans', two
'Rivers', five 'Castles' and seven 'Crabs', as well as
two Jones goods 4-6-0s and a few rebuilt 'Lochs' and
'Small Bens'. No.15012, the old 4-4-0T station shunter,
was still there but I think the photograph of her on
page 40 of 'Scottish Steam Miscellany' was one of an
engine waiting to be taken away, as she was officially
notified as having been withdrawn the same year.

At the South shed it was a case of compounds galore

144

with the welcome addition of the Caley single No.14010,
which was once more earning its keep on the Perth -
Dundee line.

Turning now to photography of moving trains, locations
near Edinburgh with plenty of interest for a Saturday
afternoon's entertainment were difficult to find.
Although numerous trains passed Craigentinny the background as well as the foreground were absolutely
featureless. To get a decent negative with slow emulsion
bright sunlight from the right angle was essential, which
ruled out westwards of Haymarket shed which in any event
was also lacking in character. Eventually Dalmeny was
found to be the answer. Trains could be photographed in
both directions between the station and Dalmeny Junction
and similarly after the junction on both the Edinburgh
and Glasgow lines. Farther along to the south there was
a change of scene where the branch line to Kirkliston
left the main line.

It was well-nigh impossible to go wrong on a nice
summer Saturday afternoon with a brisk wind from the
west. Although goods trains were few there were plenty
of Saturday afternoon specials with a good variety of
engines - in fact, there was very little on the Southern
Scottish Area that did not make an appearance at Dalmeny
on a busy weekend.

Another location for a very brief time on a Sunday
forenoon was north of Inverkeithing East box when the
line was alive with excursion trains from Edinburgh and
Glasgow to Aberdeen, Montrose and the Fife coast to St.
Andrews. They were long twelve coach trains, sometimes
double-headed by combinations of 'Directors', superheated
'Scotts' and 'Glens'. I spent a lot of time there during
1929 and the first half of 1930 and was very interested
to see later on from the pages of the 'Railway Magazine'
that the late E.R. Wethersett, a prolific railway photographer, had been attracted to these haunts of mine at
Dalmeny and Inverkeithing.

A pleasant interlude occurred at Dunfermline in the
summer. The L.N.E.R. quite frequently had rolling stock
exhibitions in aid of some charity, usually a local one,
and on a Sunday in June one was arranged at Dunfermline
Lower station. Nearby lived the Earl of Elgin, a
director of the L.N.E.R. and of the former North British,
and possibly this may have influenced the opening of the
exhibition which was undertaken by the chairman, William

Whitelaw. I was determined in some way or other to get a
photograph of him in front of his 'own' engine, No.2563
'William Whitelaw', which I knew was one of the exhibits.
It was quite a simple show with J.36 No.628B 'Byng', one
of the war service engines; a K.3 2-6-0, representing
the last word in freight; and No.2563, with a 'Flying
Scotsman' headboard. Coaching stock consisted of a first
and third sleeper, a triplet restaurant car set from the
'Flying Scotsman', a Pullman and a first and third
corridor coach, also - rather strangely - the North
British invalid saloon. As I have mentioned previously
this latter was a really fine vehicle.

Fortunately my father and William Whitelaw met frequently on church matters, so it was just a question of
introducing myself before any official intervened, which
I succeeded in doing - in spite of attempted intervention
by Major Stemp, who I believe was the operating
superintendent of the area. William Whitelaw willingly
agreed to my request, but not quite as I had wished: he
invited the entire official party to 'stand with me in
front of my own engine'. Fortunately I got another
picture less overcrowded. The plates developed nicely
and made a memory of a happy afternoon.

Our August holiday was at Kingussie and was of little
use, although we had a look at Aviemore, where there were
still several 'Lochs' and 'Small Bens'. These were
acting as pilots although some of the heaviest trains
were double-headed throughout, with 'Clans', 'Crabs',
'Rivers' or 'Castles' making very attractive combinations.

At Inverness I saw a 'Skye Bogie' in action for the
last time, No.14277 again acting as carriage shunter.
'Lochgorm' (or rather No.16119) was still to the fore as
shed shunter.

There was little left of interest in 1929 to mention
and as things turned out my days with Scottish railways
were drawing to an end with my impending departure for
Singapore in mid-June 1930. However, before then I was
able to see Gresley's high pressure (450lbs. per sq.in.)
four-cylinder 4-6-4 No.10000 fitted with Yarrow tube
boiler, which was undertaking test runs from Haymarket
shed in February 1930 not only on the East Coast line to
Newcastle but also on one occasion to Perth.

The last holiday was at Grantown-on-Spey in 1930 six
weeks before I sailed overseas. Aviemore, Dingwall,

Forres and Elgin were all visited. Aviemore still had 'Loch Laoghal', 'Loch Insh', 'Loch Luichart' and 'Ben a'Bhuird' as pilots and also Cumming's 4-4-0 No.14523 'Durn', whose main duty appeared to be a daily return trip to Perth. There were now sufficient rebuilt 'Small Bens' for the Skye line and so the 'Skye Bogies' had gone; in fact the only one left was No.14284, waiting at Inverness for her last journey south to the scrapyard. My last view of an Allan-framed engine was of No.14274 'Strathcarron' working on the Orbliston - Fochaber branch. Both the 'South American' 4-4-0 tanks, No.15013 and No.15014, were at Dingwall.

The final interesting event for me occurred during May when Haymarket, having received three new A.3 Pacifics from Doncaster, released three of her A.1s to Dundee; thus, after 24 honourable years, the Reid Atlantics ceased to be the premier engines between Edinburgh and Aberdeen.

XIII

THE FORTH BRIDGE

My affection for the Forth Bridge, going back to very early days, has increased as the years passed. It never fails to impress. The tops of the cantilever towers could be seen from my home and my brothers and I were often taken on walks to North Queensferry just to see 'The Bridge'. Opened on 4 March 1890 it was still something very new in our early family days, and those living nearby were proud of it, being well aware that thousands of others came to see what was known as the 'Eighth Wonder of the World'.

Crossing the bridge to and from school in 1915 was an adventure, especially during the 1914-18 war. There was plenty of movement in the Firth as Rosyth was the base of the Grand Fleet, and as we approached the bridge our eyes were always seeking any ship which might with luck pass directly under us - which would result in a mad rush from one side of the compartment to the other! Undoubtedly the most historic 'contact' we ever had was the super-dreadnought 'Warspite' as we were returning from school on 2 June 1916. It was not until I got home and was told that my father, who was presbyterian chaplain at Rosyth, had already gone to the dockyard that I knew that one of the Navy's periodical 'sweeps' into the North Sea had resulted in the Battle of Jutland, which had commenced on the afternoon of 31 May. Quite unnoticed by us the 'Warspite', which had been in the thick of it, had received many enemy shell hits. The rest of the evening was spent watching hospital trains on the Inverkeithing - Rosyth Dockyard branch.

It was not until 1928 that I was able to walk over the Forth Bridge, simply because 21 was the minimum age which qualified for a permit. Having signed an indemnity form, this permit was easily obtained from the office of the Forth Bridge Railway Co. in Edinburgh. The bearer had to report to the watchman at whichever end he chose to start, who would instruct him to walk facing oncoming trains to the opposite end, where the other watchman would escort him safely across the lines for his return on the other side. Leaving the footpath for any reason whatever was strictly forbidden. Incidentally, ladies were not granted permits - not at that date at any rate.

My brother and I were met at Dalmeny by the resident bridge inspector Mr. Bell, and as we started along the approach viaduct one of his first warnings was about passing trains, his advice being to turn our backs to them and to hold on to the substantial railings very firmly. Towering above us the trains were certainly very close, and the noise and vibration was tremendous. Much to our surprise Mr. Bell then suggested that we had a walk to the top of the centre cantilever.

Clearly seen from photographs, the lowest members of the cantilevers, reaching over the water from the base of the huge towers and tapering towards their extremities, are of tubular construction which allows for compression. The upper members from the top of the towers, also taper-ing, are open lattice girders which allow for tension. Access to the summit of each tower was up the long slopes on a narrow wooden pathway inside the lattice girders, which were reached by a small stairway from rail level which may be seen at each cantilever end. At first we had to practically crawl but progress became easier as the girders enlarged on their ascent to the top. On the horizontal girders at the highest point it is possible to stand inside the girders. With the latticework very widely spaced there were parts of the narrow pathway where the only safeguard from the sea 361' below was a single handrail on one side only.

Another place calling for great care was the slope up to the top, where we had to leave the safety of the enclosed pathway to climb over the upper ends of the tubes and girders reaching upwards from the bottom mem-bers of the cantilevers. There were a few steps to assist and little handrail. As I remember it the handrails on the Forth Bridge were obviously intended for bridge-minded people!

It was very quiet at the top. Trains were practically noiseless and vibration minimal. The views were splendid down river to the Island of Inchkeith and farther afield to the Bass Rock and the Law at North Berwick. To the west lay Loch Lomond and the mountains of Argyll. We would have stayed there longer but the next move was down to Inchgarvie, reached from rail level by a long straight staircase over 100' in length. Used also by defence personnel going on the island, it was splendidly fenced on both sides.

Close to the four circular granite-faced piers supporting the centre cantilever we saw the small brick pier protected by a navigation light - the only one built of eight intended to carry the central tower of Sir Thomas Bouch's proposed suspension bridge in the 1870s. Old drawings show that it would have been more in the nature of a twin bridge, with the up and down lines 100' apart. The central tower on Inchgarvie and the largest of the three would have been no less than 500' above sea level. The scheme died when the Tay Bridge went down in 1879.

Looking upwards from near sea level through the cross-bracing to the internal viaduct carrying the railway completed for us a very clear picture of the Forth Bridge in all its aspects.

The Forth Bridge has been described by many writers, but it is interesting to add a few salient details to this account of a never-to-be-forgotten day.

Promoted by the Forth Bridge Railway Co., a partnership of the North British, North Eastern and Great Northern Railways as well as the Midland, which had strong designs on a share of the Anglo-Scottish traffic, the Forth Bridge was commenced in January 1883. It was opened on 4 March 1890 by the Prince of Wales, later King Edward VII. The total length of the three cantilevers, central girders plus the approach viaducts is just under 1½ miles. Rail level from high water mark is 158', providing a clear headway of 150' for shipping. The total height of the structure as already stated is 361' above high water mark. An interesting point about the cantilevers is that whereas the centre one, which has a much longer base than the others, can be described as self-supporting, the South Queensferry and Fife cantilevers' shoreward arms are counterbalanced by weights of 1,000 tons, which can be observed incorporated in the stone arches through which the trains pass.

In 1923 the joint partnership of the Forth Bridge Railway Co. naturally was transferred to the L.N.E.R. and L.M.S., and after 1948 to British Railways.

Today the Forth Road Bridge has inevitably absorbed much of the traffic over the river, but nevertheless there has been a considerable increase in the number of trains between Edinburgh and Aberdeen as well as between Kings Cross and the north. Local services have changed in character and to mention a few regular trains to

Dundee, Inverkeithing, Rosyth, Dunfermline and Cowdenbeath now generally consist of two- or three-coach d.m.u.
sets. Trains from Waverley to Perth and Inverness,
diverted via Stirling when the line from Cowdenbeath to
Bridge of Earn was closed, once more cross the bridge,
finding their way to Perth via Ladybank and Bridge of
Earn. Dunfermline via Inverkeithing again has a good
connection with the Highlands as well as the important
town of Kirkcaldy.

The view of both bridges from the Hawes Pier at South
Queensferry is magnificent and it is fortunate each can
be admired separately, unlike the two bridges over the
Tamar at Saltash.

BRADFORD BARTON

---

publishers
of the world's largest series of
pictorial railway books
— catalogue free on request